THE
SUCCESSFUL
BOOKKEEPER

THE FORMULA TO BUILDING
A SIX-FIGURE BUSINESS & BEYOND

MICHAEL PALMER

info@purebookeeping.ca

Ordering Information: quantity sales are available on quantity purchases by corporations, associations, and others. For details, contact the publisher at the address above.

ISBN: 979-8-6862780-4-2

Cover design by Marijke Friesen
Book Designed by Doris Chung

TABLE OF CONTENTS

FREE RESOURCES TO SAFELY GET YOU TO SUCCESS!

It's hard and you know it.

The path on the way to having a successful bookkeeping business can be a scary and unsecure one.

For example, do you start every month wondering where the clients and sales are going to come from?

Do you secretly know your work is worth more than what you're charging, but you're afraid to raise your rates?

Are you working very hard in your business and burning yourself out?

The Successful Bookkeeper free resources will help you get to your goals faster and ease your worries, but not at the expense of making the mistakes so many have made before you.

To access the valuable resources, visit

www.thesuccessfulbookkeeper.com/freebonuses

to jumpstart your marketing and attract new great clients.

DEDICATION

This book is dedicated to the spirit of the entrepreneur within you. May it gain strength each day and bring abundance to you and the people that depend on you.

"When everything seems to be going against you, remember that the airplane takes off against the wind, not with it."

Henry Ford, founder of The Ford Motor Company

ACKNOWLEDGEMENT

The people around you now are essential to your success. If you get anything from this book, remember this one thing...

Don't do it alone.

I've not met a successful business person that did it alone. They had people throughout their life and business that were critical in highlighting their personal strengths and supporting them to overcome their shortcomings. In fact, the most successful people I know are masters of collaborating with others.

This holds true for anyone committed to being successful.

Like writing this book.

Without the help of dozens of people this book would have never been written let alone published and in your hands.

So, this is both a lesson and a celebration of the people in my life that helped make this book a reality.

A list of names would be meaningless to you, the reader, and there is likely a whole chapter required to do it justice to honour them all.

I would be remiss if I didn't mention my Mom, Dad and Sister because they are responsible for the foundation of my character and nurtured my heart to be open to working with and helping others. As well, Peter and Debbie for the large investment of time and the generosity of ideas they gave for me to be able to tell this story. Lastly our community of hundreds of bookkeepers that have helped to give insight into their businesses from around the world.

I'm grateful for all of their contributions and realize how much they meant to this creation process.

I also want to acknowledge all of the great bookkeepers out there, including you, for taking the time to read this book and doing the great work you do for small business.

You are far more valuable than you think.

INTRODUCTION

THE SUCCESSFUL BOOKKEEPER

"Learn from the mistakes of others. You can't live long enough to make them all yourself."

-Eleanor Roosevelt

SUCCESS

Many people speculate on the best way to increase the odds of it in business. In my experience, it's those individuals who surround themselves with successful people who have already made mistakes and found the answers. If you rely solely on yourself for the answers, you will jeopardize your chances of being your best. Looking outward is when we discover what we need and desire, and exponentially increase our achievements.

THIS IS HOW THE STORY OF THE SUCCESSFUL BOOKKEEPER BEGAN.

Her name is Debbie Roberts and when it comes to bookkeeping as a business, she reached incredible success for herself and has passed the secrets of her prosperity onto thousands of bookkeepers around the world.

I first met Debbie at a seminar she and her business coach Peter were running for their company, Pure Bookkeeping in Australia. I sensed immediately she was someone on task and well organized.

But what was it specifically about Debbie that made her so successful? She had many traits I would expect various bookkeepers to share —she was approachable yet on the quiet side, had an incredible attention to detail and was great at bookkeeping. The more I got to know her I discovered the one thing that separated her from the thousands of other bookkeepers out there in the world.

Early in the start of her own bookkeeping business, she came to a realization.She did not know how to build a successful bookkeeping business and knew she would likely fail unless she found someone that could help her find out how. Debbie had a strong desire to build a business that would give her freedom and an independent financial future. She needed the formula on how bookkeeping could be her pathway there. She was fortunate to meet business coach Peter Cook who would change her life not by giving her the formula but helping her develop it herself.

Over the decade they worked together, she would learn many things from Peter, but the most important was the conversation of value. Debbie did not value her time and she did not realize the value of the work she did for business owners.

Once Peter opened her eyes to how powerful her impact could be with potential clients, her results positively changed forever.She was now on the path towards building great systems for her business that would ultimately set her free.

If you're a bookkeeper that has a desire to have more fun, more freedom and an independent financial future then this book is for you.

In the upcoming pages, you'll learn Debbie's inspiring story and how she turned her frustrations into a high 6-figure bookkeeping business as well as other proven tips, strategies and resources that will help you no matter what stage you're on in your journey towards your own success.

Let's begin...

-Michael Palmer, The Successful Bookkeeper Podcast Host & Pure Bookkeeping CEO

CHAPTER 1

MEET THE BOOKKEEPER– DEBBIE ROBERTS

"Our deepest fear is not that we are inadequate. Our deepest fear is that we are powerful beyond measure. It is our light, not our darkness that most frightens us. We ask ourselves, 'Who am I to be brilliant, gorgeous, talented, fabulous?' Actually, who are you not to be?"

-Marianne Williamson,
A Return to Love: Reflections on the Principles of "A Course in Miracles"

Debbie's journey from humble bookkeeper to managing a high six figure business with 12 staff and then, in 2014, selling it, has all the twists and turns you'd expect from a great adventure story. It is a tale of courage, about drawing on the inner strength and confidence needed to take a leap of faith into the unknown. Like many heroes, Debbie took the road less travelled, facing obstacles both real and imagined throughout her transformative process. As an entrepreneur, there were times she sacrificed profit for experience, and times where she felt like giving up. But through all the ups and downs, trials and tribulations, experience proved the best teacher. The path to success is rarely an easy one.

Given Debbie's impressive achievements and the key mentoring role she plays today for both aspiring bookkeepers and professionals alike, it's hard to imagine there was a time when she considered dropping out of bookkeeping altogether. Like many professionals, she felt burdened by long working hours, demanding clients, and ever-changing tax policies. As she struggled to achieve balance in her life, squeezing as many hours from each day as possible, she found she simply couldn't keep up. Hiring other bookkeepers to ease her workload brought new challenges as well, as she discovered many lacked formal training. The dilemma Debbie faced was typical of any business owner; she wanted to make more money, work less, have more freedom, but couldn't risk undermining the high quality standards she had set for herself and her clients.

Debbie's journey is familiar to many. Her growing pains are ones every bookkeeper experiences, whether they choose to work as a solo practitioner or grow a team. However, despite all the bumps on her journey to success, Debbie's breakthrough moment really happened when she came to realize she had everything within her already to make the positive changes in her business. She could work smarter, not harder, and experience success beyond her wildest dreams.

Backed by perseverance and an unwavering commitment to help others, the Pure Bookkeeping System is her gift to all of us. Informative, engaging, and always practical, it is the culmination of Debbie's learning experiences. Contained within its pages is your blueprint for success. On behalf of Debbie, I invite you to be inspired and take the first step on your own journey.

THE EARLY YEARS

As a young adult, Debbie ventured into the world seeking practical work experience and a way to pay bills. She didn't set out to be a bookkeeper. She accepted an entry level position at a bank where she demonstrated a forte for organization and learning quickly. Within a few years she was promoted to accounts payable and eventually a team supervisory role. In her early 20s, she accepted her first official bookkeeping position with a gold-mining company and spent several years learning the ropes. Eventually, she decided to take a break from office work and start a family.

After two children and three years out of the workforce, Debbie began to think once again about returning to work and earning money and decided to draw upon her bookkeeping experience. Taking on a part-time role, she continued to hone her skills and gain experience. During this time, Debbie was also involved with a craft market and eager to promote her hand-made cards. Unable to find a good venue that would accept her, she scoped out an opportunity to spearhead a prestigious, high-quality market and collaborated with other skilled women. In this entrepreneurial role, she oversaw vendor quality control and bookkeeping details. For Debbie, this leadership and organizational position became a watershed moment, helping her to uncover key skills she possessed. She gained confidence and inspired those around her. She continued on this path for several years and saw the market she had created grow into the largest in the state of Victoria, eventually moving into the non-profit sector and securing new clients along the way.

AWAKENING THE ENTREPRENEURIAL SPIRIT & FINDING COURAGE

Most of us can remember a person who came into our lives and changed us forever. They held up a mirror and invited us to reflect on who we really are. When Debbie met her chiropractor and neighbour, Paul Kelly, he immediately saw her as someone who was capable of achieving great things. "Why are you working for someone else?" he asked her one day. "Why not go and get your own clients!" he urged. Flattered, Debbie took it in stride and agreed to give it some thought. But as time went on, Debbie knew he had touched upon something big. He had challenged her to think differently about herself.

"Is it really possible?" she began to wonder each time she met with him. She took stock of her current situation: three children, four day work-week, and endless family commitments to juggle. "When am I actually supposed to do this entrepreneur thing? And, importantly, what will I gain at the end?" She was at a crossroads—comfortable with where she was but curious to see what might lie beyond the horizon. But beyond all the practical concerns of leaving secure employment, another thought weighed heavy on her mind. "What if I mess things up?" At the core was fear of losing her reputation for excellence and not living up to standards she had set for herself. She didn't want to fail.

But sometimes in life, momentum takes over. With the wheels now in motion, Debbie's thirst to explore her own business was insatiable and it wasn't long before she began testing the waters. However, like many of us, she couldn't clearly see the tremendous value she possessed already as a bookkeeper. Instead of continuing on the path she was destined to take, she turned focus to individuals, helping them with budgeting. Taking this alternate path was also due to her fears around having to learn new regulations associated with GST. She didn't have the time to learn something new! Her true passion for bookkeeping was placed on the backburner. But besides searching for a compass to steer her in the right direction, there was something deeper and unresolved she needed to work through. She still had to come to terms with her deepest fears that were holding her back.

Looks can be deceiving. To most people, on the outside Debbie appeared to be thriving and pushing ahead in her new business, but a lack of confidence consumed her. She came to realize her self-limiting ideas were creating an internal struggle, impacting her self-perception and filling her doubt. She also discovered bookkeeping was her passion that couldn't be denied. Mustering up the courage to take the right step, she took an opportunity at last to help a friend, a graphic designer in desperate need of bookkeeping services.

BECOMING A SUCCESSFUL PRACTITIONER: THE CHALLENGES & REWARDS

Once Debbie was on the right path, success came strong and fast. In the first 12-18 months, referrals poured in taking her by surprise. She began to see for the first time her value and skills as a bookkeeper were highly regarded by others. But despite her growing confidence, lingering self-doubt still held her back. A key stumbling block was she hadn't truly acknowledged her own value as a bookkeeping professional. Even in the face of success, a little voice inside reminded her she was "just a book-keeper." It took everything in her to bravely keep on course.

In 2001, Debbie joined a BNI networking group that turned out to be a key career decision. Initially, networking was a new and daunting concept for Debbie. "How do I do this?" she wondered, keeping one step ahead of her fears. It was at a BNI meeting that she met Peter, a business coach, who began to learn more about her practice and offered to help her. "What is the vision for your business?" asked Peter. This was an important question Debbie hadn't thought too much about it up to that point. She still hadn't replaced her day job, though the time now felt right to take the leap. Debbie agreed to take Peter up on his offer to help once she became a full-time bookkeeper. She decided to let life normalize for a while as she made the adjustment to full-time work.

Like many talented solo practitioners, success came at a high price. Burdened with long working hours and little time for anything else, the early days revealed the pros and cons of working alone. Work-life imbalance was taking its toll. Debbie felt forced to make sacrifices and keep up a juggling act to keep family priorities and work commitments in check. She just couldn't turn away clients. Yet her confidence grew as she cleaned up her clients' "messes", and took pride in the constant referrals. "Don't give up now!" she thought. But despite her success,

Debbie was experiencing burnout. Something had to give. It was time to hire another bookkeeper.

Debbie's first experiences with hiring bookkeepers in Australia may sound like a familiar story to many. She encountered candidates who lacked formal training and qualifications. She even discovered some bookkeepers posting ads after two days of training that raised deep concerns about quality control and credibility. She had cleaned up the messes of so many other bookkeepers. How could she trust another bookkeeper with her clients? Many of the people who came did not have the skills and speed that were reflected in their resumes. To counter these issues, Debbie found herself working alongside staff she'd hired to maintain her own high standards. From notebook to computer, she logged detailed training notes. As time went on, she began to realize the toll this extra training was having on her productivity.

TAKING CONTROL: IMPLEMENTING SYSTEMS & ACTIONS

"Find your courage, change your role perception, move into business systems, and then implement action to make it all happen."
-Anonymous

Debbie and Peter decided to meet every two weeks during this critical time in Debbie's career. Together, they set personal and professional goals for her to reach. As Pete began coaching Debbie, he could see despite her growing success as a bookkeeper, she continued to struggle with self-confidence issues. Her own self-limiting ideas were holding her back from achieving her full potential. Together, they worked out some strategies to help her find the courage she would need to excel.

Defining and articulating her business vision became an important next step. From the outside, Peter could clearly see the dilemmas Debbie faced. Her cumbersome and time-consuming training process just wasn't working. Her profits suffered as she spent hours training new bookkeepers verbally, literally standing alongside them as they worked. While all her efforts were aimed at delivering consistent results to clients, a practical resolution had to be found. Debbie needed a workable system to streamline her training.

One day, Pete asked Debbie a simple question: "What if you could take the way you do bookkeeping out of your head and put it on paper? If another bookkeeper was following those procedures, could you trust them with your clients then?" Debbie was reluctant but agreed it was a great starting point, and they decided to roll up their sleeves and create a skills test.

Debbie's fears were not unfounded. One of the worst experiences she had lived through was facing an upset client whose job was messed up by a bookkeeper she had sent. At that moment, she wished the earth would open up and she could vanish. She ranted to Pete, "I quit! I'm not doing this anymore until I find a solution to the recruitment process!" She needed a solution—fast. As Debbie began to write down key testing points for job candidates, the raw bones of the data file were created. At last, Debbie was implementing a systematic hiring process, enabling her to select the best bookkeepers that could meet her stringent quality standards. As a plus, she suddenly had more time and less stress!

PURE BOOKKEEPING IS BORN

Pete continued to play a key role in other areas of Debbie's business too. He helped her work through strategies to overcome her fear of confrontation with difficult clients and set boundaries for herself and her team. Together, they got down to task and tackled the day-to-day challenges Debbie was facing as a bookkeeper. Through trial and error, new strategies for streamlining her business were revealed. How could Debbie reduce overheads? How could she find more free time but still run her business profitably?

Debbie began to document everything and, as a result, the training data files grew too. It was also during this time Peter presented Debbie with Michael E. Gerber's groundbreaking book, *E-Myth: Why Most Small Businesses Don't Work & What to Do About It*. This valuable resource literally changed her entire way of thinking about herself as a bookkeeper. She made a mental shift from seeing herself not simply as a problem-solver or technician, but as a highly valuable asset to her clients. Her value as a bookkeeper went far beyond her practical skills. The results she produced profoundly impacted her clients' success in ways she hadn't considered before. Delivering quality results by implementing efficient bookkeeping systems resulted in so much more than greater profits. She was, in fact, giving her clients access to intangible things —more time, more freedom and peace of mind.

As she began to redefine herself and frame her practice in a powerful new way, a world of unlimited potential began to open up before her eyes. Discovering her true value and creating a new definition gave her the courage she needed to move her business forward. Gerber's book had encouraged more practical and profitable approaches, changing the entire trajectory of her business.

THE PURE BOOKKEEPING SYSTEM TAKES SHAPE

With so many detailed training notes compiled and a good hiring system now documented and implemented, Debbie and Pete had some decisions to make. How could they move forward and formalize all the key ideas and data into a more practical application for training purposes? Initial plans included creating a training video but eventually both decided on a manual. Debbie asked herself, "If I were new in the industry, what would I need to know?" With this in mind, she continued to develop and refine the contents of the manual from an end-user's perspective.

In 2009, Debbie and Peter had a conversation that would change Debbie's life forever. "There's nothing really like this in the market, right?" asked Peter one day. Debbie agreed. "Suppose we created a package with different modules, such as HR, marketing and templates too." Debbie listened with curiosity. "And what if we were to run a seminar teaching bookkeepers how to avoid pitfalls and grow a successful business?" Deb wasn't particularly convinced that other bookkeepers would need or want it. She assumed that everyone would have their own systems. Pete persisted though and put his ideas on a white board. Deb left with a seed of an idea planted by Pete. After being contacted by other bookkeepers that wanted her to share her systems with them, she began to realize that perhaps Pete was right. That bookkeepers were having the same issues as she did growing her business and they didn't have detailed, documented systems in place. As her courage and trust in her own value began to kick in, she began to clearly see all that she had to offer. Much more than a training manual or compilation of her own experiences, she had created a *dynamic and invaluable system* with the power to change lives.

With a solid plan to move forward, Debbie and Peter set a launch date for 2010. As the system evolved, its contents became a culmination of learning from her own mistakes, working by trial and error. Backed by a strong commitment and desire to give it her best shot, Debbie searched for ways to continually improve and update her system.

EVOLUTION OF A SUCCESSFUL PRACTICE: THE IMPORTANCE OF COMMITMENT & COURAGE

"Let me save you the pain and suffering! If I can do it, so can you!"
-Debbie Roberts, Bookkeeper & Entrepreneur

As you can see, Debbie's transformation from working solo to running a thriving team-based business certainly didn't happen overnight. Though the eight years it took to build her high six figure business have been highly profitable, bringing personal reward and achievement far beyond what she ever imagined, the road has been a long one. For Debbie, time has revealed the mistakes made over the years, from adopting the wrong model for her business early on, to duplicating bookkeeping tasks and having too many administrative personnel. She's experienced it all. But despite the ups and downs, Debbie's transformation was only made possible by the journey she undertook.

Today, her best practices for hiring are unparalleled in the industry, and the Pure Bookkeeping Human Resources formula backed by the mantra "don't interview until they have been tested" has received awesome feedback. Debbie now benefits from a core team who are trained up to the same level, ensuring her clients get the best outcome!

AN UNLIKELY RISE: FROM BOOKKEEPER TO AUTHOR

Bookkeepers aren't supposed to write books, their job is to balance them, right? Not if you're Debbie Roberts. When Peter Cook gave her Michael E. Gerber's, *The E-Myth*, it changed her world forever. But little did she know, her vast knowledge and experiences would be documented in a book she'd eventually co-write with Gerber and Peter Cook titled, *The E-Myth Bookkeeper*. It was a terrific accomplishment for a little known Melbourne-area bookkeeper who paid many dues along her bumpy ride to success. So, how did she go from evaluating client financial data to typing words of wisdom that would assist bookkeepers worldwide?

Twelve years after Peter met Debbie, he hears his friend, Michael Palmer is organizing a conference in Canada where Gerber is the headline speaker. Peter asks Michael if he can get Gerber to sign a copy of *The E-Myth* for Debbie since she enjoyed the book. So Michael says to Gerber, "you have a huge fan in Australia" then showed him an extract of the Pure Bookkeeping System. Gerber's response blew Peter and Debbie away. Not only did he sign the book for Debbie, he then asked Pete and Deb if they would co-author *The E-Myth Bookkeeper* with him!

Debbie was literally speechless when she heard. Thus, once the book was written and published, the circle was complete. An improbable rise for a bookkeeper who never could have imagined this day would come.

Yes, anything is possible.

You can read more about The E-myth Bookkeeper at this link http://purebookkeeping.com/the-book-offer/.

CHAPTER 2

MEET THE BUSINESS COACH–PETER COOK

"You are braver than you believe, smarter than you seem, and stronger than you think."

-Winnie the Pooh

Behind every successful entrepreneur is a support system, those special people who cheer from the sidelines and celebrate others' achievements. They roll up their sleeves when it's time to help, and pick us up when we've fallen down. For many, these are our families or close friends. For others, it's a mentor whose business skills and experience we greatly admire.

Peter Cook came into Debbie's life at a critical time during her professional development. Long before collaborating on the Pure Bookkeeping project, he played a pivotal role as mentor, coach and friend, working alongside Debbie as she underwent a personal journey. Debbie's road was one that would ultimately take her to a better understanding of her core competencies while also revealing her personal obstacles, mostly psychological, that were hindering her success. Peter's second set of eyes were exactly what Debbie needed to take the right steps towards creating systems and processes that would drive her profits, and ultimately bring her happiness.

Looking back over the years, arguably Peter's most important role was helping Debbie find the courage to make it all happen. Before Debbie could experience any success, she had to build her confidence and understand the wide impact and value her bookkeeping services provided. Trusting her vision would ultimately bridge the gap between keeping the Pure Bookkeeping System a dream and making it a reality. From the early days of "Is this possible?" to the growing impact of the Pure Bookkeeping System today, Peter has been Debbie's biggest fan.

"The Pure Bookkeeping System is your blueprint to fulfilling your vision for your business whatever that is for you, but only if you want to go there. It is not meant to sit on a shelf. The question is, are you ready to take the first steps?"

-Peter Cook, Business Coach, Entrepreneur & Author

THE JOURNEY TO BUSINESS COACH

After graduating, Peter studied law and science at University of Melbourne, setting his sights on becoming a scientist or lawyer. However, like many students, his academic studies took him in an entirely new direction once he began to explore different career paths. Over time, he realized his true passion was business and made a decision to follow his heart. This foundation of practical skills and theory, combined with a natural inclination for working hard, prepared him for success in his role as a business consultant with Accenture where he spent the next several years. During this time, Peter also discovered his forte for communication and relationship building. His eyes were opened to the possibility of working for himself and he began to explore the idea of becoming a business coach. By age twenty-seven, Peter had made the transition to entrepreneur.

Being a realist, Peter knew he would be facing an uphill battle on many fronts with regards to his age and limited years of experience. He knew he would have to find the strength to face issues of perception and build his self-confidence. It's at this point Peter learned the important life lesson of persevering through challenging times and overcoming obstacles. He soldiered on, experiencing the trials and tribulations of entrepreneurial life, determined to define himself and establish a successful coaching business. Armed with a winning attitude and desire to reach his goals, success came at last. His hard work and experience were put to the test—and business boomed!

THE EARLY DAYS: PETER & DEBBIE ESTABLISH A COACHING RELATIONSHIP

Peter and Debbie's first introduction at BNI would mark the beginning of a long and fulfilling business relationship. During their first coffee meetings, Peter learned of Debbie's daily struggles as a bookkeeper. It was no wonder she had reached her full capacity; she was a full-time working mother with three teenagers at home and she was putting far more hours into her business than she needed to. There were literally no more hours in the day for her to take on new clients, let alone deliver the quality of work she was accustomed to. She needed to grow her practice but was stretched thin. Debbie agreed she could use some coaching help, and their initial ten week commitment soon extended to one year. Peter had great plans for Debbie and saw the spark of someone truly gifted and destined for greatness.

For Peter, the initial meetings with Debbie were an opportunity to discover her core competencies —detail-oriented, well-organized and very committed. But being highly valued by her clients and receiving constant referrals, it was no surprise Debbie was maxed out. Change needed to happen—fast. She needed to be in that coveted place where every entrepreneur dreams of being —working less and earning more. She needed to work smart. What was holding her back?

From Peter's perspective, Debbie was struggling with issues of confidence and trust. She wasn't ready to hand over work to others. She was a perfectionist, clinging to the idea only she could deliver the best results to clients. To add to this, she was still viewing herself as "just a bookkeeper" and maintaining the same business model and systems she always had. She was at a crossroads with wheels stuck in the mud. The good news was Debbie's open attitude towards learning and coaching were exactly the building blocks and tools she needed to move her business forward.

As Debbie's business coach, Peter had some practical decisions to make. How, specifically, could he help her? What guidance or resources could he provide to make her stronger and more focused? But before he could answer any of these questions, he needed to determine what was draining her time and energy. So with this in mind, he began to understand how Debbie was filling her days. He examined her administration models and saw areas for improvement. He discovered her biggest issues were low confidence, lack of trust, collecting money from her increasing customer list, being overworked and underpaid because she was undercharging clients.

During this time, Peter shared with Debbie his own business philosophies. To help her get her processes down succinctly and systematize her business, he encouraged her to read Michael Gerber's *E-Myth*. His rationale in doing so was to help change her mindset—to go beyond her current way of thinking and abandon self-limiting beliefs. Establishing a framework, creating processes driven by the goal of reaching success, would be a turning point for Debbie. She had to start giving priority to her feelings. After all, at the end of the day, wasn't she in the business of making her clients feel better? Her mission became to empower business owners around their finances. She started to see at a fundamental level, her bookkeeping business was really about so much more than numbers. It was about reducing confusion and fear and increasing clarity and freedom for her clients!

Debbie decided to follow Peter's advice. Adopting the principles put forth in *E-Myth*, Debbie took her first important step —she took all that was in her head and began putting it on paper. But what both Peter and Debbie didn't know at the time was the long and rigorous journey to write down her systems would take not weeks, not months, but years to perfect. Today, Peter still marvels at Debbie's unwavering focus and integrity. After all, it's not every day you come across someone so willing to take chances and apply themselves so wholeheartedly to their vision!

REMOVING BARRIERS TO SUCCESS: STREAMLINING DEBBIE'S BOOKKEEPING BUSINESS

"Recognize that there will be failures, and acknowledge that there will be obstacles. But you will learn from your mistakes and the mistakes of others, for there is very little learning in success."
–Michael Dell, Chairman & CEO of Dell

How to improve her bookkeeping business became an ongoing inquiry. Debbie faced new challenges and wondered daily how she should move forward. What mistakes was she currently making in her business? The nature of Peter and Debbie's relationship focused on Peter testing her limits at every opportunity. His "go for it" attitude pushed her out of her comfort zone to face difficult decisions and scenarios. Soon Debbie was having conversations with clients she had always avoided —late payments, sub-contracting projects or breaking agreements. Each triumph brought the reward of personal growth, and her confidence became like a muscle strengthening with practice.

She had come a long way since her days of executing the books solo and being exhausted with the onrush of customers pouring into her one woman practice. Recognizing she needed help, she'd take a crack at hiring. It had its extreme lows, but eventually would get better. With

Peter's sage advice, she'd figure out how to hire quality bookkeepers that would lift a huge burden off her shoulders.

A key step in streamlining Debbie's business was to reduce her administration costs. Up to this point, after assembling a good-sized staff, she enlisted the help of a supervisor to oversee junior bookkeepers to ease the workload created by having to continuously check work herself. However, a closer look at this model revealed her profit margins couldn't support it. She was paying up front costs for hours spent on non-bookkeeping duties before billing clients. Putting his coaching skills to work, Peter established several key performance indicators (KPIs), which included paying bookkeepers only for their bookkeeping time (not administrative tasks) and implementing a more automated billing process. Debbie began to see how many hours she was paying for that weren't billable to clients.

Ruthless monitoring of her business ensued. As a team, Debbie and Peter paid particular focus to billable hours, with a goal to maximize efficiency and profits. Each mistake brought new learning opportunities and decisions to be made, ultimately paving the way for Debbie's success.

LEARNING TO TRUST HER VISION

"Am I on the right path?" After about three years, with so much work put into her system, Debbie began to question her direction. Should she go back to where she started? Author, Michael E. Gerber reminds us this type of questioning is common to many small business owners. They reach a plateau where they need to move forward but fear and indecisiveness take over.

Over the years, Peter had watched Debbie grow both personally and professionally, demonstrating unwavering commitment as she recorded her systems. "Do you know you have developed the best bookkeeping system in the industry?" he asked one day. He had been doing his own industry research and his findings had fallen short. *There was simply nothing else that came close to what Debbie had developed.* How could Debbie have *any* doubts she was on the right track? Was it she hadn't fully realized her vision for teaching and empowering other bookkeepers? Peter knew Debbie's system was different. Her system had the potential to transform the bookkeeping industry.

By 2009, revitalized with a new sense of purpose, Debbie and Peter set Pure Bookkeeping on a new course, one that would eventually open doors for thousands around the world. But they still had a lot of work ahead of them. Like any successful partnership, they forged a foundation of trust that began with mapping out each other's roles and responsibilities with respect to the project. Peter brought to the table the necessary entrepreneurial mindset and marketing expertise to make it happen: "This is what you could do, and this is what it could look like!" They committed themselves to working through any issues that might arise and went forth with complete transparency. They set out to win!

EARLY SUCCESSES: THE PURE BOOKKEEPING SYSTEM

Peter and Debbie placed great importance on getting Pure Bookkeeping off the ground with minimal cost, coming up with creative and cost-saving ways to market their new system. A key strategy centered on establishing a price point for Pure Bookkeeping that would offer an excellent alternative to costly franchise setup ($40,000 plus). Investing in Debbie's proven system, one tested on literally hundreds of clients, for a fraction of the cost, made perfect sense even to the most cautious bookkeeper!

Other strategies involved offering incentives for early adopters and running pilot seminars. But Peter and Debbie knew there would be no shortcuts to getting the Pure Bookkeeping System off the ground. It would take tremendous effort, dedication and good old-fashioned elbow grease. And most importantly, success hinged on both partners believing 100% in the value Debbie's system would bring to others.

It wasn't long before they found their first customers and celebrated their achievements. Comments from early adopters were music to Debbie's ears and confirmed everything she had hoped her system could offer others: "This system is invaluable! You could triple the price and the investment would be a fair deal!" Pure Bookkeeping provided motivated bookkeepers with an opportunity to access all of Debbie's years of experience, right in their back pocket!

According to feedback, Debbie's unique system, which is based on 15 years of growing her bookkeeping business, solved 3 key problems for bookkeeping business owners:

1. Lack of proven marketing strategies to grow your business
2. Lack of detailed and documented bookkeeping systems
3. Lack of proven HR systems for you to recruit great bookkeepers

But, on top of all the practical advice and applications was something perhaps even more valuable, something Debbie and Peter hadn't considered at the time. Her system gave bookkeepers insight into the knowledge they already possessed. Hers was a system that could instantly empower bookkeepers with a renewed sense of confidence and credibility. This was gold.

"What will it take to transform the industry?" Peter and Debbie wondered in these early days. They decided to set the benchmark at 1,000 Australian bookkeepers adopting their system.

MAKING THE COMMITMENT & FOLLOWING THE PATH TO SUCCESS

"The Pure Bookkeeping System will make it easier and quicker, but is not a replacement for hard work. You must do the work to be successful and apply the systems."

-Peter Cook

You may be thinking, "Debbie sounds like a superhero. Could I do it too?" If you're committed to your business and its growth, passionate about the bookkeeping profession and open to learning, the answer is yes! You will overcome whatever you need to overcome. Like Debbie, Peter reminds bookkeepers of the importance of assessing one's commitment to growing your business before making the leap. This step is crucial. Out of 10, are you a level 6 or 10? While it's normal to be level 6 in some areas of life, running your business is not one of them!

As Canadian author, John Warrillow reminds us in his influential book *Built to Sell*, don't set out to build a job—build an asset that produces wealth. Articulate your own vision for success. Only *you* can decide your future outcome. You CAN create an extremely profitable asset.

Today, Peter continues to be inspired by Debbie's total commitment to continuous improvement and updating of the Pure Bookkeeping System, even when she ran her own business, BACS Bookkeeping. As their business coach/client relationship continues to grow, so does the industry-wide impact of their project in Canada, UK, Australia and beyond.

Pure Bookkeeping has helped facilitate change in profound ways, namely by helping bookkeepers embrace the full value they offer.

CHAPTER 3

WHERE ARE YOU NOW?

"Your life does not get better by chance, it gets better by change."
-Jim Rohn

You are about to embark on the journey of your life and you've got all the tools you need to reach your destination. But are you ready to take the first steps? The stories Debbie and Peter shared remind us anything is possible when courage and hard work are put to the test. If you know where you want to go, you CAN make it happen. Our goal is simple—we want you to benefit from the best tools available today in the bookkeeping industry. However, these tools alone will not be enough to get you to the finish line if you don't know where you want to go. Only when you are ready to become a successful bookkeeper, and put all of Debbie's experience to work for you, will these tools take you where you want to go!

Now is the time to ask yourself a simple question. Do you want to take this journey to become a successful bookkeeper? Only you can define your business goals and change your mindset to prepare for success. Right now you have an opportunity to change your direction. What road will you take? Keep in mind, starting from the place you are right now, at this moment, you will have the points, maps and compass to reach your destination faster. You have everything you need to avoid the common pitfalls and setbacks all bookkeepers face. The Pure Bookkeeping tools are exactly what you need to keep you on course. We hope you will take the first steps on the journey of a lifetime!

UNDERSTANDING YOUR BARRIERS TO SUCCESS

Everyone is at a different place on their bookkeeping journey. You may be part way there at this moment, or you may just be starting out. But no matter what stage you are at, trust that NOW is the time to take stock of what is working in your business and what is not. What are the barriers preventing you from being successful? Do you have all the tools you need right now to go further and faster? If not, what are you missing? Identifying the factors that have been holding you back from reaching your full potential is an essential first step on your journey towards becoming a successful bookkeeper.

EVERYONE HAS PSYCHOLOGICAL BARRIERS THAT ARE DIFFICULT TO OVER-COME.

They hinder one's attempts to become more successful and more profitable. They can include any or all of the following:

- Fear of failure (What if my business doesn't work out?)
- Lack of confidence/courage (I'm not sure I have the ability to be successful)
- Perceived lack of support (I need help but I don't know how to get it)
- Fear of hiring the wrong people (They can't produce the quality I expect)
- Fear of change (If I do things differently it won't work out!)

Do any of these challenges sound familiar? Facing our fears is difficult. But even more problematic is the decision to leave our issues unresolved, hoping things will work out over time. Doing so is leaving our success to chance. Have you ever felt resigned to your business? When things haven't been going well, it's easy to accept you've "hit a wall" and can go no further. If you've experienced feelings of apathy or indifference towards your business, perhaps one of these psychological barriers underlies the problem. Progress is only possible when we confront the issues we've been avoiding. For most of us, however, living with feelings of dissatisfaction can be more comforting than facing our obstacles head on.

WHY DO THESE PSYCHOLOGICAL BARRIERS EXIST?

Arguably, there are many forces that shape our personalities and the career paths we choose. However, I believe many of the problems entrepreneurs experience, bookkeepers included, stem from feelings of not being in control. Fear and uncertainty become the default when we are not in control of the direction our business is heading. Every bookkeeper needs to know how to run their business and measure the results of success. Confidence comes from knowing the direction you want your business to go and how you plan to get there. It's easy to bury your head in the sand and hope you're on the right track! If a challenge needs to be addressed, it will only become more difficult over time.

Like all entrepreneurs, bookkeepers are at their best when their business systems work. In other words, when the best practices and systems for hiring, marketing, administration and communication are in sync, business thrives. When a business owner feels empowered and in control, every aspect of business from hiring to strategic planning comes into sharper focus.

HOW DOES THE PURE BOOKKEEPING SYSTEM HELP?

Debbie's system was designed to tackle many of the psychological barriers we've identified. More than a "how to" guide, Pure Bookkeeping offers a powerful new way to run your business that builds confidence and keeps you on target to reach your financial goals. Because every facet of your business is detailed and explained, backed by proven systems to help you build a great asset, fear and uncertainty are greatly reduced. You no longer have to face the unknown.

ARE YOU ANOTHER DEBBIE?

Peter asked Debbie one simple question—"if you could clone yourself, how would this change your relationship to hiring others?" Peter could see Debbie was a perfectionist. She had set high standards for herself and her clients. How could anyone live up to her expectations? The underlying assumption Debbie had was others would not be able to follow her stringent guidelines or implement the quality control measures she expected. Her first attempts at hiring other bookkeepers confirmed her beliefs. She experienced the frustration of managing underqualified staff. She began to add up the hours she was wasting training and cross checking others' work. As much as she needed to expand her business and create a team of bookkeepers, Debbie began to question whether it was all worth the headache. Maybe she should just go back to working solo.

ARE YOU SOMEONE WHO HAS HELD BACK OR NOT HAD THE PROPER DIRECTION TO SHOW YOU THE WAY?

Peter could see the methods Debbie used to hire new bookkeepers were not working. She was a bookkeeper who had no training in HR. Because of that, her "interview" technique was more like a chat over coffee. The process was high-risk and time consuming. As a small business, she didn't have the "on-boarding" system that larger businesses had. It's no surprise she came to the conclusion maybe she was better off working by herself. She needed help. When Peter and Debbie realized specific ways they could improve her hiring process, they worked diligently to create a testing system and put measures in place. Consequently, as Debbie approached her hiring practice in a more systematic way, her confidence grew and her team of qualified staff grew too. She used leverage to her advantage, hiring once, training once, and generating profit over time.

CREATING A MILLION DOLLAR PRACTICE

"If you can dream it, you can do it."

-Walt Disney

Have you ever felt you were not living up to your full potential? Peter could see Debbie was a diamond in the rough. She had the determination, abilities and mindset to be successful. Debbie just needed the right tools to get there. She required systems that would maximize efficiency and profits and minimize overhead costs. She needed to work smarter, not harder, and bring balance to her life.

The journey we are talking about in this book is NOT about making small improvements to your business; it's about creating a profitable asset that is saleable. It's about helping you make the mental shift towards how you think about yourself as a bookkeeper and the value you provide to your clients. But first you need to be clear on what your business model will be. Will you be a *successful business owner* or a *successful sole practitioner*? There are some important distinctions between these two models.

Let's examine both:

SUCCESSFUL SOLE PRACTITIONER

- You earn close to a six figure income
- You work a 40 hour work week and charge healthy rates
- You provide great service which is highly valued by a loyal client base
- You have great systems in place for marketing and bookkeeping

SUCCESSFUL BUSINESS OWNER

- You are earning a six figure plus income
- You no longer have to do the books and run the business
- You have a team-based practice with 2-3 plus bookkeepers
- You have great systems in place for marketing, bookkeeping and Human Resources
- Your business is an asset that can be sold for 1 to 1.2 times revenue

Notice there are some similarities between these two models. For both, success is built on having great systems in place that make daily operations smooth, measurable and profitable. Also, there are loyal clients willing to pay top rates for excellent service. However, there is one key difference: if you leverage these things as an individual (sole practitioner), you will leverage SOME profit, but not as much as you actually could. The business owner will always leverage substantially more profit—often for working fewer hours.

Bottom line is if you are a successful sole practitioner, you may be earning great money but essentially you have created a job for yourself. In other words, there is a ceiling on the number of hours you can work and how much you can charge. Your business is worth about .25 cents to the dollar. In contrast, a business owner is able to leverage much more profit and thus have a significantly higher business evaluation. Let's do the math: bookkeeping businesses are bought and sold all the time, typically for 1 to 1.2 times revenue.

CREATING LEVERAGE: MOVING FROM TECHNICIAN TO ENTREPRENEUR

"We cannot solve our problems with the same level of thinking that created them."

-Albert Einstein

Are you in business because you're a great technician? Many professionals, bookkeepers included, have excellent technical skills but this doesn't translate into being adept at growing a business. While many may seek the trappings of owning a business, such as enjoying greater profits, more vacation time or reduced working hours, the reality is they remain a technician. This is because their business simply doesn't have the framework to evolve in a way that will yield greater returns. They haven't created leverage, meaning systems that are scalable and repeatable that will drive their profits.

This is a Bookkeeping Business Journey Matrix image below that displays what happens when you apply leverage, what it does to your profit and where it can catapult you.

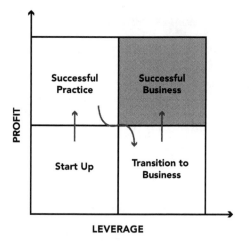

CREATING BUSINESS LEVERAGE IS A KEY COMPONENT OF THE PURE BOOK-KEEPING SYSTEM.

But what exactly does this mean? We can think about leverage in a number of ways. In the physical sense, leverage involves making use of a tool or mechanical device (i.e. a lever) as an assisted advantage to lift or move another object. Leverage allows us to use an existing mechanism and maximize force for the purpose of easing a task.

In business, leverage has a more metaphorical meaning:

"The ability to influence a system or an environment in a way that multiplies the outcome of one's efforts without a corresponding increase in the consumption of resources. In other words, leverage is the advantageous condition of having a relatively small amount of cost yield a relatively high level of returns."*

In a bookkeeping practice, leverage is created by implementing systems that are clearly delineated, easy for others to follow, and repeatable. For example, Debbie's compilation of training notes for new bookkeepers evolved over time into a training manual. Every bookkeeper that Debbie hired had the advantage of following her clear instructions and methods, thus increasing the quality of output (and minimizing feelings of frustration!) Creating a "how to" guide became a time-saver for both Debbie and her team. Debbie was able to reduce hours spent training and cross checking others' work and, as a plus, experienced greater confidence knowing her team could now deliver consistently strong results. With a loyal team following a streamlined method of bookkeeping, expectations are clear and everyone benefits. Increased employee retention is the best way to sustain your bookkeeping business for years to come.

COMMON PITFALLS OF STARTUPS

For most of us, changes in our lives happen out of desire or necessity. In every successful business, there comes a point when it is time to expand and take on more clients. However, a key dilemma many startups face is there is no leverage and profits in the early stages which can be catastrophic. They are not great marketers or managers and therefore make a lot of mistakes. In their desperation to grow, they end up working for the worst customers and charging far less than they are worth. When a sole practitioner transitions to business owner, they advertise for help and take the risk of a new hire not working out. Rarely are pro-active steps taken to systematize the hiring process and communicate business expectations once a new member is on board. Measures and benchmarks for success are non-existent which leaves much to chance. From the employee's perspective, trying to understand what is expected can be frustrating and demoralizing. In short, the chance to establish a positive and profitable business relationship fails.

Would-be entrepreneurs feel the negative repercussions of not creating business systems every day. When a business owner hasn't established systems for others to follow, they are quickly perceived as not being in control. Consequently the business runs the risk of becoming people-dependent. The business begins to evolve NOT based on the owner's ideas and expectations but on the actions and initiatives of employees. With no one steering the ship, it floats aimlessly. Before long, the resulting confusion of a people-dependent business leaves the business owner longing for the old days when they worked alone. Add to this the mounting costs of transitioning to a business, including leases, equipment and more, and it's not uncommon to see profits drop at this phase.

FOLLOWING YOUR MAP & STAYING ON COURSE

What Debbie learned in her transition was ultimately success depended on creating systems that were easy for others to follow and understand. Becoming a systems-dependent business was a clear goal Peter set for her. Why just hope your staff will do better? YOU are in control! You are the only one who can set benchmarks. Over the past several years, I have talked to many bookkeepers who have gone through the experience of hiring other bookkeepers who didn't work out. They went back to working solo. Perhaps this has happened to you too.

This part of the journey, transitioning from solo practitioner to business owner, is where your compass becomes most important. Experiencing setbacks and steering off course are normal for all entrepreneurs. The goal of the Pure Bookkeeping System is to learn how to do everything BETTER and transition into a successful business.

FIRST STEPS OF YOUR JOURNEY

"When obstacles arise, you change your direction to reach your goal; you do not change your decision to get there."

-Zig Ziglar, Motivational Speaker, Author & Salesman

\As you can see, Debbie didn't jump from bookkeeper to operating a high six figure level business overnight. She also didn't begin her business with twelve bookkeepers and five weeks holidays. She experienced her share of mistakes and obstacles on her path to success. She also experienced the highs and lows of anyone who has ever worked hard to realize their dreams. But what she did create was something invaluable to every bookkeeper who follows in her footsteps —a map to cover ground faster and further! As we continue together on this journey, we will explore Debbie's business path in detail and discover what she learned at each step. It is our sincere hope the Pure Bookkeeping System will give you the compass and foundation you need to help you reach your desired business goals too, and build the dream practice you envision.

We are here for you. Good luck!

CHAPTER 4

WHERE DO YOU WANT TO GO?

"To the person who does not know where he wants to go there is no favourable wind."

-Seneca, Philosopher

Do you have a vision for your future? Now is the perfect time to imagine, create and prepare for a brighter and more prosperous tomorrow. I invite you to open the floodgates to the possibilities in your life. Will your business look the same one year from today or will it be completely transformed? Remember all the tools you need to make the necessary changes and step into the future you desire are in your hands.

From the place you are right now to the place you want to go will be made that much easier with the points, maps and compass you can create with the help of this book.

In Chapter 3, we discussed the importance of looking inside yourself to assess where you are. We also learned knowing your destination before setting out on your journey is essential. Taking first steps in any direction won't get you to the finish line. I also encouraged you to take a personal inventory of your strengths and weaknesses so you could better understand your own barriers to success. Do you now feel more committed to exploring new directions? If you are feeling more resolved to move forward and walk the path of the successful bookkeeper, congratulations! This just may be the best decision you will ever make.

As you may have realized by now, this journey isn't just about achieving your financial goals. What we are really talking about is creating a future rich with possibilities which includes spending more time with your loved ones and doing other enjoyable things that nourish your soul. Your happiness *and* prosperity are really what Debbie's journey can teach you. But before any goals can be reached, some fundamental changes will have to happen on the inside. Only YOU will be able to shape your future through visualization and decision-making and determine what success means to you. In this chapter, we'll discuss how powerful the mind can be when we make a committed decision to change the direction of our lives.

CHANGE YOUR MINDSET, CHANGE YOUR LIFE

"Dissatisfaction and discouragement are not caused by the absence of things but the absence of vision."

-Anonymous

It's a human trait that we are more likely to overestimate the capabilities of others and underestimate our own. As we look around at those who are successful and accomplished, we make assumptions about how much stronger and smarter they must be. For some bookkeepers, Debbie's story may seem too unrealistic to relate to. The assumption is her good fortune must come down to her being more capable, better organized or more outgoing. But where does this thinking come from?

We all have filters through which we view the world. Our filters are unique and reinforce beliefs we have about ourselves, often at a subconscious level. Everything we see around us, we view in relation to our learned understandings about who we are and what we are capable of achieving. For example, your filter may be just like Debbie's was at one time: "I am just a bookkeeper" or "I'm not an entrepreneur." The unfortunate part is most of us cling to these self-limiting beliefs for years—sometimes forever—until we have the strength to question our self-perceptions.

If you're ready to take the first steps on this exciting journey, you must begin to change your mindset. This starts by acknowledging any negative and devaluing ideas you have about yourself and realizing they are simply untrue. Your self-assessment is wrong. The ideas you've held strong for so long are a mental construct. If you really want to change your life, your challenge will be to move beyond your current mindset to make change possible. But this is not an easy task. The self-limiting ideas we have run deep, often stemming from our earliest experiences with failure. Failing at something and having that failure acknowledged by others makes a long-lasting impact. We carry the burden of our own negative self-perceptions, struggling with them whenever we face something new. However, the good news is anyone can make a decision to change his/her mindset. Our minds are much more powerful than we realize!

Exercise 1: Look around the room you are in. Make a note of all the man-made objects you see.

Take a look at your list. Consider everything you've noted. Everything synthetic you see was created by someone at some point in the past. Every object began with someone's idea of what that object should be like and how it should be constructed. Why is this so important? Everything we see was *first* created in the mind. In other words, reality is created by our thoughts. But it's not just what we see beyond our doorstep; our lives are created in the same way too.

Exercise 2: Look at your life today. What are 3 things you have achieved you once thought were impossible? (i.e. an award, owning a home, reaching your education goals, working from home etc.).

From the time when you hoped and dreamed to where you are right now, something happened. What actions or engagement did you personally undertake to facilitate the shift from dream to reality? At this very moment, you are living the life you have visualized. Your thoughts and mindset are directly responsible for the achievements you have noted.

CREATE THE FUTURE YOU ENVISION

From the perspective of where you are right now, what does your future look like? Will you be working fewer hours, enjoying more vacations *and* making more money? If you're like most hard-working bookkeepers, these goals may seem out of reach at the moment. Trying to achieve a sustainable work/life balance as you squeeze every minute out of your day leaves little hope for change to happen. Now take a moment and try to visualize your future in the most desirable way possible. Let go of all hesitation and make every effort to really think about what you want. What would your ideal life look like? Will you be working as a remote bookkeeper managing your own schedule and clients? Will you have a reliable and loyal bookkeeping team like Debbie's to build and drive your profits? Now is the time to give shape to your dreams.

Take a moment to check in with yourself. Think about any emotions you may have experienced while visualizing your ideal future. Perhaps you felt some hesitation. Maybe you heard that little voice inside reminding you of what is possible and what is not. This is totally normal. After all, those self-limiting thoughts have had control for some time! There is absolutely no reason why your future can't look like Debbie's. Her path from humble bookkeeper to owning a profitable practice was also filled with hesitation and uncertainty, the very same emotions you may be feeling right now.

Today offers the chance for fundamental changes to begin happening in your life. While there are many unknowns about the future, one thing is certain —it will arrive. Time waits for no one. You and everyone you know will experience change. Why not create an awesome future for yourself? Just as your past thoughts and ideas shaped the place where you are right now, how you think today will bring you into your next chapter of your life.

Exercise 3: Your future is shaped by what you think. What are 3 things you used to dream about but gave up on? Are these things you want to bring back to your future?

Everyone is faced with choices and we've already learned we step into the future through our thoughts and actions. With this in mind, only you can make a decision about what you want to reenergize and commit to as you move forward. Think about what you truly desire, being as honest as you can with yourself. This exercise isn't about what other people would like you to do. It's about revisiting dreams from your current perspective, the place you are right now. What's still important to you? What dream did you give up because you thought it just wasn't possible? While it's perfectly fine for our dreams to change over time as we are exposed to new life experiences, I encourage you, the bookkeeper, to step up and open your mind and heart to dreams that are still waiting to be discovered.

In 2002, Deb's big dream was to replace her husband, Neil's income, so he could retire by 2010. In 2012, he dropped down to 4 days per week and was able to retire in 2014. It took 4 years longer than she planned, but does that mean she failed? Of course not. Was she convinced that she would be able to replace Neil's income when she set her goal? No. But, it was so important to her family that she believed it was possible and that was enough to keep her moving towards that goal.

DEBBIE'S LEAP OF FAITH: FROM DREAM TO REALITY

It's hard to imagine there was a time when Debbie could not visualize a different future for her business. Yet with a seemingly never-ending amount of work to do, likely thinking about how to change her direction wasn't high on her to-do list. Like many bookkeepers, she was focused on the micro day-to-day operations. While she hoped one day she would work fewer hours and have a reliable and skilled team, she wasn't clear on how it was all going to happen. Her destination was still unknown.

Until she sold her business in 2014, Debbie operated a successful bookkeeping business, backed by a proficient team. She also plays a key role as mentor and educator for other bookkeepers. So what were the roots of change that made it all possible? For Debbie, a time came when she could no longer ignore the barriers that were holding her back. She had to make a decision to change her mindset and come to terms with the filters that were preventing her from seeing her own potential. When Peter began coaching Debbie, he facilitated these changes. He helped her understand the statement "I'm just a bookkeeper" needed to be replaced by one more powerful: "I am a highly valuable bookkeeper who is an asset to my clients." Her lack of confidence about the value she offered and her entrepreneurial abilities were making positive change virtually impossible. She had to alter her mindset to create the future she desired.

Debbie's mental shift set the wheels of change in motion. With Pete's help, she was now ready to tackle the important questions you are also likely asking yourself right now. What did she *really* want from her bookkeeping business? How could her business run more smoothly and profitably? What kind of money did she want to earn? With Peter's coaching help, Debbie was able to define her goals for the first time. With her destination clearly in sight, and a powerful new mindset, Debbie could take on the world! The next steps would be creating the points in the map to take her efficiently from Point A to Point B and, fortunately for the rest of us, devise the blueprint for the Pure Bookkeeping System she continues to develop to this day.

UNDERSTANDING YOUR CORE VALUES

"When your core values are in line with your life vision, the journey is far more enjoyable and the likelihood of getting there much greater."
—Marilyn Atkinson, Coaching Visionary, Author and Entrepreneur

Ask yourself a simple question —why do I want to take this path to success? Each of us has a set of core values that underlies every decision we make. These fundamental beliefs are unfaltering and steer us in the right direction. For example, core values may reflect the emphasis we place on the importance of family, or keeping a work/life balance. It's also common for companies to have core values that all employees can uphold (i.e. honesty, respect, and optimism). Importantly, everything we choose to take on in our lives should, ideally, be in alignment with the values we subscribe too. Long term happiness and satisfaction can only be achieved when goals and values are in harmony. Let's examine this concept more closely:

Exercise 4: Think of 5 experiences in your life that made you happy. Now try to recall what it was about these experiences that brought you happiness.

Everyone's core values are unique. They inspire and drive us. For example, you may recall I place great value on the importance of travel. Because my core values include being open-minded and learning from others, travel brings much happiness and satisfaction. For some, thinking about life's happiest moments may bring to mind buying their first car or watching a family member graduate from university. Maybe it was seeing a friend win a medal or reach a goal that seemed unreachable. In all these milestone moments, happiness is a reflection of core values.

Next, take a moment to think about the opposite scenario: when have you been unhappy in your life? Do you know *why* you felt that way? Experiencing unhappiness or dissatisfaction is often the result of our core values not being aligned with our actions. For example, many of us at some point have experienced a sense of remorse that comes with mismanaging money. It may be the time that money set aside for a much-needed vacation was used for something else. It could be the time money was spent needlessly on an impulse purchase. In these cases, the core values of managing resources well or maintaining a good work/life balance were not aligned with actions. Identifying our past or current struggles is a useful way to shed light on our values and what we need to do be happy.

Now take a look at your life today. What is bringing you happiness? Try to determine the positive experiences in your daily life that are aligned with your core values. It may be as simple as the satisfaction you get from being totally organized or setting and achieving weekly goals. In these cases, your core values of commitment and achievement are reflected (and will be a tremendous asset on your journey toward becoming a successful bookkeeper!) Keep in mind it is only through the alignment of core values you will come to the point of action and begin the shift away from any stress or discomfort you are experiencing. Alignment is the key that will open the door to a happier future.

DEFINING YOUR GOALS

Now it is time to define what YOU need to be happy as you prepare for your future. Think about your short and long term personal and business goals and let your core values guide you. As we discussed in Chapter 3, a key question you must ask yourself is —will I be a successful practice or a successful business? Let's review the two different career paths you can take:

SUCCESSFUL SOLE PRACTITIONER

- You earn close to a six figure income
- You work a 40 hour work week and charge healthy rates
- You provide great service which is highly valued by a loyal client base
- You have great systems in place for marketing and bookkeeping

SUCCESSFUL BUSINESS OWNER

- You are earning a six figure plus income.
- You no longer have to do the books and run the business.
- You have a team-based practice with 2-3 plus bookkeepers.
- You have great systems in place for marketing, bookkeeping and Human Resources.

Your business is an asset that can be sold for 1 to 1.2 times revenue.

Another way to measure your business success is through a belt system. Like martial arts, you go through different classes and focus on different things. Here's a table to explain a bookkeeping business or practice.

Belt	Revenue	Focus	Team Members	Days You Work
Black	$600,000 - $1M+	Exit	10x	0
Red	$500,000	Service	8	0
Blue	$400,000	Management	6	2
Green	$300,000	Human Resources	4	3
Yellow	$200,000	Marketing	2	4
White	$100,000	Bookkeeping	1	5

WHICH ONE IS *YOUR* FUTURE?

Being certain of what you most desire and what you are ready to commit to is top priority. Total honesty is the key. If you are feeling uncertainty about your direction, the time to explore your concerns is now. But don't be disheartened if the idea of becoming a successful business owner seems overwhelming. While it may be intimidating, this future is totally within your reach. *Other bookkeepers just like you are pursuing their dreams as we speak.*

As you give thought to your future, keep in mind the filters we discussed earlier. Try to see through any smoke screens which may be self-created. Ask yourself practical questions during this process of self-reflection —do I want to work from a home office? Do I want to charge premium rates? Is my end goal to establish a saleable business? Give yourself permission to dream big!

GET READY FOR THE ADVENTURE OF YOUR LIFE

So far we've looked at where you are right now. We've also worked through where you want to go next. This brings us to perhaps the most important piece of the puzzle which is commitment. How committed are you to embarking on this journey toward becoming a successful bookkeeper? As Debbie discovered, setting clear goals to manage a system-based profitable business required her 100% commitment.

As we continue on this journey, we'll continue to clarify your business goals including creating a Mission Statement for your business. Debbie and Peter have a mission to transform the bookkeeping industry by helping great bookkeepers grow their businesses. What will your mission be and how will you define success? The sky is the limit as you begin the process of visioning your business and articulating the unique value and contributions you will make.

CHAPTER 5

COMMITTING TO YOUR MISSION

"The world steps aside for those who know where they are going."
-Anonymous

Ever notice how doors just seem to open and obstacles clear the moment we become committed to something? The resources and support we need to reach our goals suddenly appear. Commitment is a powerful mindset that is at the heart of everything we set out to accomplish. From the moment we commit to be and achieve our very best, every decision becomes easier and our dreams are that much closer. You may recall Debbie could only move forward and grow her business once she was fully committed to her vision. Her new mindset gave her the strength to move according to her own compass. Moreover, everything she needed to be a successful business owner, from finding new clients to establishing networks, became plentiful.

I can't stress enough the role of commitment in reaching your goals. Why is this? Your personal path for success must be firmly grounded in commitment or you will run the risk of taking your life in any direction other than the one you want to go. In Chapter 4, we discussed the importance of looking inside yourself to see what path is right for you. I invited you to let go of that inner voice holding you back and open yourself up to possibilities—to think big and imagine a brighter and prosperous future. Now is the time to assess how committed you truly are to the future you've envisioned. This is a crucial first step. From there, you will be able to create a Mission Statement that speaks to the unique value you provide as a bookkeeper and, most importantly, find the words to communicate that mission to your customers.

HOW COMMITTED ARE YOU AT THIS MOMENT?

Any dream that ever came true since the beginning of time began with someone's commitment to something important. History books are full of examples of influential figures committed to greatness and change. You only need to look at the achievements of Gandhi, Martin Luther King, Jr., Nelson Mandela or the late Maya Angelou, just to name a few. We can all think of individuals we know and admire who have made a difference in this world by committing themselves to such worthy causes as humanitarian improvement or environmental awareness. Positive change, big or small, can make a huge difference in the world. How many products and services that you use today began with someone's idea to make things better? The point is each of us must make a decision to commit to the future we want—one that brings positive change for both ourselves and those around us. Which future will you choose?

Below is a scale that shows commitment level on a scale of 1-10 (10 being the highest). This scale can apply to anything in your life right now, such as achieving work/life balance, taking a vacation this year, saving for your child's education, or retiring by a certain age. If you are at level 10, this means you are completely focused and unwavering in your commitment. (Congratulations on knowing what you want!) The question I encourage you to explore now is whether you are completely committed to creating a profitable bookkeeping practice. How easy is it for you to say those words right now? Where are you on this scale?

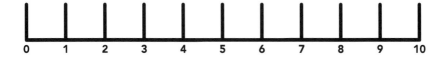

If you are not a 10, now is the time to ask yourself why. What is holding you back from being totally committed? I'd like to share an observation I've made over the years working as a business coach. In my experience, many professionals have trouble distinguishing between commitment and fear. When I ask clients to assess their commitment level, just as you are doing now, they hesitate. They will reluctantly admit they are an 8 or even lower. When I ask them about that gap between where they are and fully committing, they inevitably tell me it's because they're not sure they can actually achieve their goals. They simply don't know how to do it. Because they have reservations about their own abilities, they believe they are not a 10. Can you relate to this struggle?

Another reason why bookkeepers are reluctant to commit is because they think that being 10/10 committed requires them to work full-time. The typical demographic of a bookkeeper is a mom with small children and their priority is their family. And they think they can't be 10/10 committed to their business while they have small children. What Pete says in the Australian Pure Bookkeeping seminars is that they can be 10/10 committed for the time they have available. So, if they have to work school hours 3 days per week then, for that time, they are 10/10 committed to their business. When this is explained it is quite liberating for them to know that they can do both.

KNOW THE DIFFERENCE BETWEEN FEAR & COMMITMENT

Fear is an illusion created around what factors might make you unsuccessful. What fear is actually doing is clouding your judgment around your ability to understand how committed you truly are. It's important to remember commitment is a mindset and it is not the same as fear. A low score that reflects fear of uncertainty or lack of knowledge about how to achieve a goal, is NOT the same as a low score due to low commitment. The exercises in this chapter are about assessing your commitment and putting all other factors aside. There will be lots of time later to assess the "how to" and nuts and bolts of planning your next steps later. Now is the time to commit to your business vision and develop the mindset to be your very best.

DECIDE WHAT JOURNEY YOU WANT TO TAKE

Remember, early on Debbie had her fair share of fears holding her back from growing her business. She wondered, "How can I do this?" and "How can I juggle all my family commitments and be successful?" Peter could see Debbie had big dreams and a lot of concerns but never once did he question her commitment. Having worked with other entrepreneurs, he could see commitment wasn't really the issue. Debbie was struggling with the fears shared by many such as the fear of failure and how to overcome hurdles. As her business coach, he played a key role in helping her let go of the psychological barriers that were causing her to question her commitment. Debbie soon began to see her lack of confidence and feelings of uncertainty were directly influencing her ability to achieve her business goals.

So far, we've talked a lot about the journey to become a successful business owner. However, it's possible right now you are questioning why you aren't totally committed to being a business owner. You may discover you are not committed to growing a business. That's perfectly fine! The question I would challenge you to think about is what ARE you committed to? Recall in Chapter 3 we examined two very different business models —Sole Practitioner and Business Owner. While there are key differences, it's important to understand each of us has a preferred path. You can certainly be very successful and satisfied pursuing either path. Be honest with yourself. If being a successful sole practitioner means your business and life goals will be fulfilled, that's the future you should pursue. Making the right decision now will save you disappointment later. Sitting on the fence is not an option! All that truly matters is you embark on the business journey that is right for you.

According to Deb, the other reason why it's critical to be clear about which path you are committed to is that every decision you make after that will support that choice. If you aren't clear then your other decisions will be difficult. Also, you could recommend that, if you aren't sure which option to choose then you should play the bigger game. You can always change your mind when you get to a successful practice and stay there however you will have set up your business with the goal in mind to grow a business with staff which will make it more valuable.

OVERCOMING OBSTACLES THROUGH COMMITMENT

"Until one is committed, there is hesitancy, the chance to draw back, always ineffectiveness. Concerning all acts of initiative and creation, there is one elementary truth, the ignorance of which kills countless ideas and splendid plans. It is this: The moment one definitely commits oneself, then providence moves you. All sorts of things occur to help one that would never otherwise have occurred. A whole stream of events issue from the decision, raising in one's favour all manner of unforeseen incidents and meetings and material assistance, which no person could have dreamed would have come their way. I have learned a deep respect for one of Goethe's couplets: Whatever you can do, or dream you can do, begin it. Boldness has genius, power, and magic in it. Begin it now."

-William H. Murray, The Story of Everest

Everyone has a personal story of commitment, one of overcoming obstacles and facing fear. A time in their life when the switch just turns on and magic happens. I'd like to share mine with you. I grew up in the Okanagan Valley, a beautiful area about five hours drive from Vancouver. Every year, for 25 years, this area has hosted the world-renowned Ironman triathlon. This challenging race requires athletes to swim for 3.86km, cycle for 180km through the mountains then run a further 42.2 km. Growing up, I watched athletes compete, each year asking myself "how do these people do it? I could never complete this race!" I didn't relate to myself as an athlete and was never really good at sports. However, in my early 20s, my best friend Brent began to train for the triathlon. The more I watched, the more I began to think differently about myself. I began running and getting in better shape. Soon I was swimming and biking too.

While watching Brent competing in his 3rd Ironman I bumped into my high school gym teacher. He asked, "Palmer, you ever think you could do one of these?" and I answered "no." But secretly I said "absolutely! I'm going to run an Ironman in two years." Something clicked right at that moment. My mindset changed and I was committed. I set a personal goal and knew I would achieve it. Importantly, I hadn't gone into training with an athlete's mindset. I had to change my way of thinking to prepare for success. Even in the face of numerous hurdles along the way, the help I needed miraculously appeared. When I suffered knee problems, I found the right therapist to push me through. I even met the right coach who helped me improve my performance and keep me accountable. I surrounded myself with people who were going in my direction. I became committed and as a result performed beyond my wildest expectations! I learned while my commitment was tested hundreds of times along the way, my desire to achieve the goal gave me the strength to persist and succeed.

DEFINING YOUR MISSION STATEMENT: WHAT IS YOUR REASON FOR EXISTENCE?

You may be familiar with the idea of creating a personal mission statement. This is a statement that reflects your values, objectives, and the life roles you assume. Through self-reflection, you consider the larger context of your life and who you really are. A personal mission statement can play a key role by keeping you on track and avoiding actions that do not align with your core values. Similarly, a business Mission Statement comes from understanding your business purpose and how it relates to the overarching goals you have.

Once you feel certain you are fully committed to your journey to become a successful bookkeeper, your next step is to determine what exactly you are committing to. Defining and articulating your Mission Statement lays the groundwork for moving into the planning stages of your business. So, where do you begin?

A good Mission Statement answers a need. It is developed in that space that lies between where your customers experience the greatest "pain" in their business and where they want to be. It is why your business exists. Your services will fit somewhere in the spectrum and provide a win-win for both you and your customer.

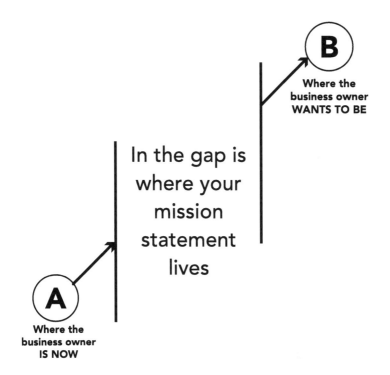

The first step is to ground yourself. What does your customer need from you? Understanding the crux of what business owners need and how your services answer that need is a key first step in formulating your Mission Statement. In my experiences, every business owner I ever coached desires three basic things —financial success, more freedom and less working hours. Every business owner got into business to fulfill one of these three things and has varying degrees of success in accomplishing them. These reasons are likely why you went into bookkeeping too! A practical way to think about this is to imagine what pain a business owner experiences when they don't have a great bookkeeper. Put yourself in their shoes and imagine the worry and anxiety they must feel every moment of the day.

Living with worry, frustration and sleepless nights becomes their reality. What about their employees? What impact does bad bookkeeping have on them? Consider the wider impact bookkeeping messes can have on families and communities. From this standpoint, you can begin thinking about where businesses want to be.

What is the gap that exists between Points A and B? This is the gap you must close as a bookkeeper. Imagine win-win scenarios for your clients. This is the place where you will develop your Mission Statement. As an exercise, reach out to a few of your customers and ask them what they think makes a successful bookkeeper. What's their definition? What pain have your bookkeeping services taken away? There you will find your purpose and value.

Debbie's Mission Statement is to empower business owners around their finances by removing confusion, fear and uncertainty and replacing it with clarity, freedom and control. How did this statement evolve? Recall that for eighteen months, Debbie lived through the experience of helping businesses clean up the "messes" left behind by other bookkeepers. She had insight into the catastrophic consequences of bad bookkeeping. Clients came to her literally in tears with a big mess to fix. These rescue jobs left her disillusioned. She couldn't trust other bookkeepers to perform well and, as a result, was stuck and unable to grow her own business. Her Mission Statement is a reflection of the needs she uncovered during her work. Her mission became to positively impact the wider demographic, from business owner to community and beyond. By empowering business owners around their finances, she could reduce confusion and fear and better everyone's lives.

LIVING & BREATHING YOUR MISSION STATEMENT

Your Mission Statement underlies every aspect of your business. How you market yourself and how you network will come down to your mission. What language will you use to communicate the value proposition you present to business owners? Consider the following statements:

"We take care of your finances so you can take care of your business."

"We audit proof the financials for your business so you can rest easy."

Notice both of these Mission Statements fill that gap between A and B—the place where a business owner may be now with their bookkeeping and where they want to be. The words in these statements resonate with business owners. Who *wouldn't* want to have their financials audit proof? That's exactly what they are seeking.

Let's take another example. The Pure Bookkeeping mission is to transform the bookkeeping industry by helping great bookkeepers grow their businesses. Our Mission Statement evolved as we met with bookkeepers and began to understand their pain. In what ways does this statement speak directly to bookkeepers? What is the gap Pure Bookkeeping is filling? The idea behind this Mission Statement is we have a goal to help bookkeepers realize the true value of their services and the widespread impact they can make on businesses and their communities. Importantly, this Mission Statement also speaks to my core values as a business coach and entrepreneur, namely the importance I place on empowering others to become top-performers. I believe successful businesses are the catalyst for positive change in our society.

Where will you go from here? At this moment, you are surrounded by everything you need to be successful. Will you change your mindset to create the future you have envisioned for yourself? Some might call it the Law of Attraction, the idea that like energy attracts like energy. If you put your positive energy towards what you want, you will likely achieve it. In many ways this is true. However I believe that achieving personal success really comes down to knowing what you want, staying totally committed to your goals and taking the actions in line with your desired outcomes. Being positive is crucial, but commitment will always make the difference between success and failure.

CHAPTER 6

GOAL SETTING FOR SUCCESS

"If you go to work on your goals, your goals will go to work on you. If you go to work on your plan, your plan will go to work on you. Whatever good things we build end up building us."

-Jim Rohn

Every person that ever achieved great success started where you are right now. They committed to their vision and worked out a plan to get to the finish line. But they didn't simply work hard, they worked towards a goal—a totally different experience. Look around you right now. Do you ever wonder why so many people seem to be working hard yet feel adrift? They are lost because they have no clear direction for their lives. Tony Robbins reminds us, "Setting goals is the first step in turning the invisible into the visible."

What are your business goals? How do they reflect your life goals? Understanding where you want to go and how to get there can seem overwhelming. Psychological barriers can get the better of us. Earlier I encouraged you to let the creative dreamer side of yourself take over. We can learn a powerful lesson about the importance of dreaming and imagination from one of the most original minds of the 21st century, Walt Disney. In his view, there are two types of individuals that work in any organization, the innovative and the practical. Both, by definition, are at odds with each other; the dreamers are the driving artistic force while the practical are concerned with implementing or the "how to" part. With this in mind, Disney made a point of separating the creative folks in his own business, so the dreamers would always dream big. Can you imagine how easy it would have been for a character concept like Mickey Mouse to be laughed at? Mice are not lovable! People are scared of mice! The iconic Disney symbol, instantly recognizable worldwide, would never have been. What might have happened if the creative and the pragmatic had been working in the same space? Consider how such an analogy plays out in your life. Does your inner critic step in the moment you begin dreaming?

Last chapter we discussed the importance of developing a strong Mission Statement and committing to it. By now, you've likely got a better sense of the direction you'd like to take your business and your life. Now you need to get specific about the goals you will be working towards. There are two parts to this puzzle —a) what specific goals do I want to reach? and b) what are the steps to get there? In this chapter, we will explore how to look at the road ahead and how to begin setting your goals. I invite you to keep an open mind and think outside the box as you embark on this important next phase.

NOT ALL GOALS ARE CREATED EQUAL

As a business coach, one of the biggest problems I see my clients struggle with is goal setting. For many, there's a lot of anxiety around imagining the future and planning. "But how will I do it? What are the steps?" These are the first questions that come up when envisioning the future. An internal drama unfolds as the dreamer and practical self fight for their turf. Just as the bar is raised, the critical voice takes over. The only way to break through is to consciously decide to put judgment on hold.

From an early age, we become familiar with the idea of setting personal goals. We work towards milestones such as getting accepted to university or saving enough money to buy a first car or home. We've all been taught different approaches by our teachers, family and friends and there are endless print and online resources to help us set goals. My belief is a clear goal has a much greater chance of being realized than an ambiguous one. Organizing your time and resources in the most effective manner leads to greater efficiency and more positive outcomes. Ironically, I've also discovered those who adopt a system for setting goals suddenly have more free time to enjoy life, even though they are accomplishing far more than they ever imagined! Less running around means less wasted efforts.

My approach in this chapter is to explore SMART goal setting, a term coined over 30 years ago by George T. Doran in a paper submitted to *Management Review*. Today, it remains one of the most widely used and well-documented goal setting systems and for a good reason. From project management to personal development, the SMART approach ensures the best outcomes for achieving success.

SMART is an acronym for a 5-step method which outlines the criteria to set goals. Different sources use the letters to refer to different things. The core idea is to bring together objectives and action plans:

SPECIFIC

- Can your goal be stated in one sentence? A specific goal means you can easily answer all "W" questions such as Who, What, Where, When, and Why. For example, what do I want to achieve and when?

MEASURABLE

- How much? How many? How will I know I'm on the right track? A measurable goal means you know exactly where you are at any time on your path.

ATTAINABLE

- Is your goal one that can be achieved given your current life situation and mindset? Can it be accomplished?

RELEVANT

- Does your goal reflect your larger life goals? Is this the right time? Is it worthwhile and desirable?

TIME-BASED

- Is there a timeframe and deadline for your goal? What will you do today? How about one month from now?

Because they are specific and measurable, SMART goals significantly increase your chances of success. Consider these two goals, one general and one specific: a) I want to lose weight b) I want to lose 10 pounds over 8 weeks working with my personal trainer. Notice the specific goal answers key questions and is linked to information. This goal indicates who is involved (the trainee and trainer), the specific accomplishment (lose 10 pounds), and time constraints (8 weeks). Elaborating on this statement, it becomes easy to determine other aspects of the goal such as place, purpose and benefits. In contrast, the general goal of losing weight provides no action plan or framework. It only expresses a hope the pounds will be shed at some point. Being too general is the most common pitfall when setting goals.

Now let's look at some business goals that likely apply to your life right now. If you've created a Mission Statement and are feeling totally committed, now you are ready to articulate your goals. Consider these two statements: a) I want to grow my bookkeeping business b) I want to grow my bookkeeping business by 25% this year. While both statements are results-oriented, the second contains parameters for profit growth and deliverables. We know where the finish line is and when we'll arrive. Now let's take a closer look.

PUTTING YOUR SMART GOAL TO THE TEST

Example: "I want to grow my bookkeeping business by 25% this year."

Suppose this is your actual business goal. Are the "W" questions answered? What is actually being communicated and how specific are the parameters? To start, what dollar amount does 25% growth really represent? Obviously this figure will depend on one's current income. Always push yourself to be specific and indicate amounts, as they'll be easier to measure later. Where will you be running your business and will your work environment change? Adding location is important. Any planned changes to your current work setup may require you to adjust your growth target; for example, plans to work and travel abroad introduces factors such as time zone changes, technology (internet access) or even the challenge of adjusting to a new culture. Finally, what does "this year" really mean? If a goal of 25% growth is set in April, are you giving yourself eight months to achieve it or a full year (April to April)?

HOW DO YOU MAP YOUR SUCCESS?

Let's say the above goal is now specific and you feel confident and excited to move forward. Now what? Your next task will be to work from macro to micro, breaking down your large goal into smaller more manageable components. In other words, your large goal will have a subset of goals which, when achieved, will bring you closer to your larger goal. Recall in earlier chapters the importance placed on having a vision and compass. This process of goal setting is laying the foundation and following the steps that will take you on the right journey. Your road to success, however, you have defined it through your goal setting, will be clear when you've laid the plan.

This part of your bookkeeping journey, working through the details and determining the small steps, can feel daunting. There are so many choices to make. What will you do in the first week, first month or first quarter to reach your goal? Here is a simple brainstorming activity to get you started:

Exercise 1: Imagine you have already achieved your goal: "I want to grow my bookkeeping business by 25% this year." All your hard work has paid off and you're at the finish line. What accomplishments got you there? Work backwards. What specific goals and steps did you take to bring you to this point? Focus on core activities rather than details. For example, some initiatives might include:

- I joined a networking group and contacted 20 new prospects
- I launched a new bookkeeping newsletter
- I used a system for hiring and training and brought a bookkeeper on board
- I created Value Bundles for my bookkeeping services
- I upgraded my skills to widen my service offerings
- I started a bookkeeping blog on my website which attracted five new clients

Visioning success is a technique often used by top athletes. Sometimes thinking about your journey from this standpoint, looking back on the road you've travelled, can help to reduce anxiety and uncertainty around what steps to take. When Pete and Debbie began working together, they got down to task setting goals for her business. One of her objectives was to manage more clients without adding more working hours to her schedule. She realized the only way she was going to achieve this was by leveraging the talents of a great bookkeeping team. Being able to visualize her goal was a key part in moving forward with the arduous task of documenting an effective system for hiring and training the best bookkeepers.

Exercise 2: Continue brainstorming and let your creative juices flow. The next step is to take your list above and break it down further. How *specifically* did these steps bring you closer to your goal of growing your business by 25% over a one-year period?

Some examples of *specific steps with specific financial results* include:
- Contacting 20 new prospects enabled me to secure 5 new clients ($10,000)
- My bookkeeping newsletter resulted in 2 new clients ($4,000)
- Value Bundles helped me add on average 5% to each client's project ($3,500)

Hint: Try this exercise working with a specific dollar amount as indicated above. If 25% growth translates to $20,000 net growth, how theoretically could this growth be realized? The more realistic your answers, the more useful (and motivating) the exercise will be.

HOW DO YOU MEASURE YOUR SUCCESS?

An integral part of setting goals is ensuring tools are in place to measure your performance. You should know at any given step how close you are to achieving your goal. What will your yardstick be? Obviously, the larger the goal, the more complex the measurements will be. Many consider tracking one's success the most important aspect of goal setting because it is intrinsically linked to motivation. Having criteria to measure results makes goals real and tangible. I like to think of measurements as milestones—accomplishments to be celebrated. Milestone achievements are a reflection of your focus and integrity.

Assume the list of accomplishments described above became actual goals towards growing your business by 25%. Applying measurements takes us back to using SMART goal setting criteria and answering the "W" questions. For example:

Goal: "I want to contact 20 new prospects and profit $10,000."
Specific questions:
- How will you contact them and by what date?
- How many new clients (from the 20 new prospects) are needed to generate $10,000 annually?

In this case, you might break down the goal and set measurements for success in the following ways: a) secure 3 new clients by June b) generate $5,000 in new projects within 6 months c) contact 10 new prospects by February, etc.

BENCHMARKS ARE WHAT COUNTS

I always caution my clients around the pitfall of measuring specific goals without tracking. Progress happens in incremental steps and everything counts. Consider how Debbie's life changed when she set a goal to start networking. As a result, she met her coach Peter. From there, her goal to become a successful entrepreneur came into sharper focus and was that much closer. If someone sets a goal to lose weight then steps on to the scale and sees no results, this does not mean he or she has failed. In this case, while the major outcome is important, what counts are the finite actions such as making better breakfast choices or taking stairs instead of elevators that put someone on the right track.

SET ATTAINABLE & REALISTIC GOALS

Nothing is more frustrating than setting out on the greatest adventure of your life without giving yourself the best chances for success. A wonderful aspect of goal setting is you can become totally objective in the process of imagining your future. With a clear goal in sight, you can begin to see everything has to change or improve for you to obtain your goal. *How can you expand your current thinking to bring a far off goal into sharp focus?*

What lies between you and your dream? From this perspective, you can consider potential roadblocks.

Do you need to adjust your current work schedule? Do you need to cut down on volunteer or extra-curricular activities? Perhaps you have no dedicated quiet workspace to work on your goals. Should you complete more courses or achieve certification to open up more opportunities? When a goal you truly desire is within reach, you will be unstoppable! Harness that energy to move mountains.

STAY COMMITTED OR READ JUST YOUR TARGETS

"Though we may have desires or bold goals, for whatever reason, most of us don't think we can achieve something beyond what we're qualified to achieve. Why, I ask, do we let reality interfere with our dreams?"

-Simon Sinek, author of *Start with Why: How Great leaders Inspire Everyone to Take Action*

"Why" is one of the key "W" questions that SMART goal setting invites us to explore. WHY do you want to achieve your goal? The desire to reach a goal should always align with our core values. Even though it may seem obvious to want to grow your bookkeeping business, understand all your reasons for doing so. Does growing your business mean you will have more money to travel? Will creating a saleable bookkeeping business enable you to retire earlier and fulfill another dream you have? Questioning your commitment can happen at any stage. Be sure growing your bookkeeping business is relevant to the life goals you have. Are you willing to consider a wholesale change to the way you currently approach your work? What is non-negotiable?

Successful goal setting hinges on honesty and knowing what's best for you. Embrace your goals! Remember, your goals that require you to do the work you love are always the easiest to achieve.

CHAPTER 7

BREAKING THROUGH SETH GODIN'S DIP

"Most competitors quit long before they've created something that makes it to the top." ·

–Seth Godin, *The Dip: A Little Book That Teaches You When to Quit*

You've defined your goals. You've created your Mission Statement. Now what? A strange thing happens to many of us on our journey to success. Just when things are going great, we have a set back, run into our barriers or fall into a slump. Suddenly, our dreams seem just out of reach and all we want to do is walk away. We want to give up on our goals… even though they mean the world to us. "What went wrong?" we ask ourselves. "Why should I keep going?"

Seth Godin in his New York Times bestseller *The Dip: A Little Book That Teaches You When to Quit (and When to Stick)* was the first to recognize this predictable pattern so many entrepreneurs fall into. In his book, he examines the importance of identifying this dip, or slump, and what it takes to get back on track. While most people will experience moments of doubt, it's important to trust the upward swing *will* happen if the mindset to succeed is strong. There's a popular notion that "quitters never win, and winners never quit," but Godin reminds us the opposite is in fact true. Winners quit all the time. They just quit the right stuff at the right time. The secret is knowing the difference! Being totally committed to being the best bookkeeper you can be right now will be your key to helping you regain your focus and energy later so you can get past the dip.

The greatest challenge you will face on your personal path to success is overcoming the urge to settle for average. Staying the course and moving beyond mediocre takes strength and confidence. If you are excited by the long-term potential of meeting your goals then try to avoid getting caught up in a difficult moment. The test is to push through and not default to what feels safe. Often it's our self-sabotaging thoughts that get the better of us. Words such as, "maybe this is as good as it gets" or "I should be happy with what I've achieved" can send you on a downward turn. It's easy to start feeling comfortable when average becomes your new normal. To a large extent, staying on track depends on how well you plan your journey. Did you take the time to create well-defined steps? Did you take your first one *only after you felt totally committed?* Perhaps some steps were skipped or you ran into unforeseen obstacles and the road ahead is now unclear.

In this chapter, I'll show you how you can identify your own slump, or dip, and explore strategies to help you get back on track. Remember you are not alone. The dip you might experience will likely be one that has tested many a dream seeker before you. Importantly, we'll also take a closer look at the underlying patterns of thought and behavior that contribute to feelings of doubt. The desire to give up at this critical stage is all too common. I believe by first getting a handle and greater perspective on the psychological barriers that may trap you into a mindset, you will be able to apply some practical tools and techniques to break through and surge ahead.

"THE DIP"

Going through a dip is unsettling. Just having a bad day can be trigger. Losing business to a competitor or having to apologize to a client can send you into a tailspin. Yet this dip can also be subtle—so much so you may not even be aware of that little voice inside reminding you can back out at any moment. You can still walk away from your dream and go back to how you used to work. Fear and uncertainty can swiftly take over and for many bookkeepers they do. So what happens when you default to the status quo? If you let the chips fall so-to-speak, what you've really done is made a decision NOT to have control over your future.

In Chapter 4, we discussed the importance of mindset in creating the future you imagine. Clearly defined goals backed by a positive attitude will take you where you want to go. If you are living in survival mode, stressed and uncertain about your goals, the mind is set on keeping everything afloat. Any drive to make more money, gain more freedom or carve out a future that inspires you will only happen if you change your mindset. At this very moment, you are at a critical time in your bookkeeping journey. There are pitfalls that are bound to test you and self-limiting beliefs that will shake your confidence. Recall that for Debbie, the idea of quitting bookkeeping altogether was something she considered during her own times of struggle. Fortunately, Peter was there to coach her and help her stay the course!

"I'M NOT MEANT TO SUCCEED AT THOSE THINGS I'VE BEEN DREAMING ABOUT."

As we begin to give energy and direction to our dreams, this is the point where the negative self-talk can happen. With the first steps come the first challenges. These might include financial (can I survive and pursue my dream?), emotional (I don't have the strength to face failure), or even physical (I feel too drained to go on). Many don't push through to the next phase. Feeling indecisive and lost, hurdles are seen as insurmountable. How can they possibly overcome them? Many can't get out of the dip and so they return to where they were before.

So what *do* you do if you feel like you're not progressing? My best advice is to take a breath and come back! Ask yourself some basic questions to better understand what's really happening with your business. What's at the heart of your struggle? You began your bookkeeping journey with a detailed plan. This is your roadmap of where you want to go and how you will get there. What happened along the way? Try and identify the obstacle you ran up against. Looking back requires an analytical eye. Strive to put your emotions aside and be objective. Discovering a misstep, pinpointing where something went wrong, is not about focusing on failure. It's about being proactive and empowering yourself. Always give yourself permission to regroup and move forward. Put another way, you are repositioning yourself for success. For example, you may realize you skipped some steps because you didn't follow your marketing plan. What was the one thing that still needs to be done? What component will bring everything together? Get some help if you need it. Remain objective and open to adapting your plan. Perhaps your marketing tasks are too detailed or your short-term goals unrealistic. Timelines and parameters you set were not achievable. Take some time to review your goals to make sure they are SMART.

ARE YOU A STORYTELLER?

Breaking through mindset barriers begins with articulating WHAT the barriers are and REDEFINING them in a new context. We all tell stories based on what we've learned from others or what we've personally experienced. But perhaps the most important story we tell is our own. What is your life story? What have you learned to believe about yourself? For most of us, our story is formed early on in life and stays with us forever. It defines who we are, what we can and cannot do. Our story is about what we're really good at and where we always fail. Sometimes the story sounds something like this: "I'm great at math but can't draw anything," or "I'm not an athlete. I was never good at sports." Each time we communicate these ideas, out thoughts are reinforced, thus perpetuating a vicious cycle of self-limiting beliefs.

Recalling past failures is a painful experience. Dwelling on negative episodes where we've let ourselves down contributes to low self-esteem or feelings of inadequacy. Interestingly, this often happens at the worst moment—just as we are about to embark on a new journey. Suddenly the stories we've been telling ourselves for years are louder and more difficult to silence. Remember when Debbie set out to grow her bookkeeping business and the words she repeated to herself were "I'm not an entrepreneur!" Up to that point, her story was about being "just a bookkeeper," not a successful business owner. In order to redefine herself and imagine a different future, she would have to change the story she was so used to telling! Coming to terms with those events in your past that may be contributing to self-limiting beliefs is a crucial step to getting through a dip. Remember, these past beliefs are false. All it takes is the right mindset to overcome them.

GAIN CLARITY BY REMOVING BARRIERS TO SUCCESS

Below are some exercises to help you get a better understanding of what may be holding you back. By identifying the self-limiting beliefs you have at this very moment, you can begin to take steps to change your self-definition. Use the chart below to create a Commitment Plan.

Exercise 1: What are the beliefs you have about yourself that are getting in the way of your success? Place them in the first column.

Exercise 2: For each belief, create a contrast statement that will negate it. Place in second column.

Exercise 3: Now go one step further and create a Commitment Statement. This action-oriented step will help you make the transition into a more positive mindset. What action will you take to reinforce your NEW belief about yourself? This action will also redefine how others see you too.

Self-limiting Belief (Negative)	Contrast Statement (Positive)	Commitment Statement
Example: I don't have time to reach my goal (secure 3 new clients this month)	I have 1 hour a week to work on my goal	I will work 1 hour per week to reach my goal by organizing an email and phone campaign to introduce my bookkeeping services to local businesses

MOVING BEYOND SURVIVAL MODE

"Our self-image and our habits tend to go together. Change one and you will automatically change the other."

-Maxwell Maltz, Surgeon & Author

"I can't get to my goals. There's no time in my day!" Sound familiar? Many professionals who set out to make great changes to their business often fall into a trap I refer to as "survival mode." In this state, an individual begins to express issues around accessing his or her goals. They find themselves in this predicament for any number of reasons, many of which are psychological. I'd like to share a story about a client of mine (let's call her Theresa) who found herself in such a state. Though totally committed to growing her bookkeeping business, she was living in a constant state of anxiety, mainly due to financial uncertainty. She was focusing on all the little things, yet in the process was selling herself short. Her fear and struggle had become so overwhelming she didn't know how to begin even thinking about her business goals. She didn't have the peace of mind or the resources to move forward.

One day I asked her, "What are you trying to survive from?" Working together, we began to identify and pare down those things that were making her feel stressed. What thoughts preoccupied her mind? She began to realize she was living in constant fear of not being able to pay her bills. Since any move towards business growth carried risk, she was stuck in the present. How could she get control over her worries and move forward?

A basic understanding of the human brain in layman's terms helps explain how survival mode impacts us. Broadly speaking, our brains are divided into three parts, Reptilian, Mammalian and Visual Cortex, sometimes referred to as the "three brains." The reptilian brain is the oldest part designed through evolution to keep us alive and is responsible for fear, freeze and the "fight or flight" instinct. When we feel anxious or stressed, we engage this part of our brain. In contrast, the Mammalian brain's primary functions include emotions, memory and regulating the body's response to sensory information. The visual cortex (neocortex), or so-called thinking part, is what enables us to visualize the future—a distinctly human trait.

In the case of Theresa, her thought patterns were actually keeping her in survival mode. Her ongoing stress and drive for self-protection was engaging the reptilian part of her brain. It was impossible for her to move forward. Her only choice was to find a way to free herself from her current way of thinking. Only by gaining a new perspective and freeing herself from constant worry could she begin to align her activities with her goals.

"You can conquer almost any fear if you will only make up your mind to do so. For remember, fear doesn't exist anywhere except in the mind."

-Dale Carnegie, Author & Speaker

A key part of coming to terms with our deep-seated fears is to visualize and articulate all the possible scenarios we think could "kill" us. What are the events that could happen on your way to achieving your goals that would be devastating? *By isolating your fears, you no longer perpetuate the loop of fear that makes you feel trapped.* In Theresa's case, her fear was linked to money. But what specifically was the money issue about? What was the gap? As it turned out, her sole focus on survival (paying her monthly bills) forced her to only think of making money in the short term. In her mind, she had rationalized that aiming for short-term results would minimize future risk. However, with this mindset she was unable to focus on the future she desired. She could not keep focused on her commitment because she felt trapped.

TAKING A PRO-ACTIVE APPROACH TO OVERCOMING FEAR

Have you come to terms with all your "what ifs"? Sometimes a contingency plan is all you need to help you relax and face your next steps with confidence. In Theresa's case, she discovered having some money set aside to cover two to three months' expenses was all she needed to feel more relaxed and unblock her mind. This security would give her some wiggle room in case she experienced a dip. Exploring the "how to" part (how to get these funds) became a simple next step once her fear was isolated. She could finally put her worries to rest and calm her mind. As you pursue your own journey to success, consider how you will face your own fears and insecurities along the way. Like so many before you who have chased their dreams, you too will find the strength and a way forward.

CHAPTER 8

10 MISTAKES BOOKKEEPERS MAKE

"Learn from the mistakes of others. You can't live long enough to make them all yourself."

-Eleanor Roosevelt

Over the past several years I've had the opportunity to meet many successful bookkeepers that have shared their own stories of struggle. Just like Debbie, they endured the trials and tribulations common to all bookkeepers. Some faced roadblocks early on in their careers while others began to stumble after several years of running a successful practice. Most often, mistakes were attributed to poor systems or having no system in place at all. In other cases, failing to effectively market their services or establish a lucrative fee structure led to weak returns. Many made mistakes at the critical point of transitioning from sole practitioner to team-based bookkeeping.

As part of Pure Bookkeeping's commitment to helping great book-keepers grow their businesses, I'd like to share with you *10 Mistakes Bookkeepers Make in Business,* a downloadable resource created with expert guidance from Debbie herself. Based on her own vast experience, Debbie brings a sharp perspective and wealth of knowledge to the key issues all bookkeepers face, regardless of where they are in their careers. In this chapter, we will review some of the most common mistakes so you can begin to build awareness around typical pitfalls and, most importantly, take action to avoid them.

MISTAKE #1—UNDERCHARGING

Undervaluing bookkeeping services is a rampant and recurring problem in both the UK and North America. Like many skilled freelance profes-sionals, bookkeepers are notorious for undercharging their services. Why is this? Most bookkeepers go into the bookkeeping profession with the understanding there are employer expectations around fees. Once their business is established, they ask an employer, "What would you like to pay me?" Naturally, business owners respond in a way that most benefits them —they negotiate the lowest rate possible. Sadly, this has become the norm and bookkeepers are vastly underpaid.

This problem arises partly from the fact bookkeepers view themselves as technicians. They are being paid to provide error-free reports on time. Their clients have also come to view them this way and historically have paid low fees. Unfortunately, many bookkeepers lack business experience and may not realize the tremendous value they provide to the business owner. The truth is excellent bookkeepers are the key to business sustainability and growth. Did you know the average Canadian bookkeeper charges $35-45 hour? This fee is not even on par with low-skilled and non-specialized service providers. Consider the amount charged for cleaning services or even getting an oil change —likely double! Earning more money begins with changing your mindset around value. You will never have a successful business or practice if you are not charging the value you deliver.

MISTAKE #2—BOOKKEEPERS THINK BUILDING A BOOKKEEPING BUSINESS IS ABOUT DOING THE BOOKS

"I'm just a bookkeeper!" These are the words that went through Debbie's mind when she struggled with the idea of becoming an entrepreneur. It seems many bookkeepers believe they are just performing bookkeeping tasks, yet this couldn't be further from the truth. "Doing the books" involves doing key tasks that are intrinsically linked to every business decision a client will make. The future of a business depends heavily on what information and financial opportunities a bookkeeper uncovers and communicates.

I cannot stress enough the importance of changing this self-perception so you can reframe your life's work in a whole new way. The first step involves making the mental shift from thinking of yourself as merely a technician to a valued service provider. Bookkeepers help business owners actualize their vision and become successful. The key takeaway is business owners thrive because YOU provide impeccable books! From there you can begin to think differently about what you can offer and charge accordingly for your services.

The most valuable person in the company is the one who handles the finances. A business will *only* reach its full potential with a good bookkeeper. Case in point is the story of Janet, a friend of mine who today owns several restaurants and attributes much of her success to the expertise and excellent advice offered by her bookkeeper. Janet was running a popular Yorkville restaurant when her bookkeeper brought to her attention the excessive costs she was incurring due to food purchases and spoilage. Because her bookkeeper had extensive experience in the restaurant niche, she was able to give Janet reports and key insight into industry standards, benchmarks and comparables. In turn, this information helped inform her to make decisions on how to run her restaurant more profitably. As a result, Janet learned how to purchase goods more efficiently, tighten her labor costs and increase productivity. Today, Janet is an absentee owner who is thriving and enjoying more time to do what she loves. Ask Janet today how she did it and undoubtedly she'll say it was her great bookkeeper that made all the difference.

MISTAKE #3—NOT DOING ANY MARKETING

When bookkeepers fall into the trap of thinking of themselves as merely technicians, they tend not to market their services. The perception is marketing is only for companies who need to establish a brand or sell something. Marketing is about advertising so it doesn't apply to bookkeepers. For the most part, bookkeepers see themselves as non-marketers. Many don't have the know-how or perhaps even the confidence to market their services. Yet the changing nature of today's business world makes marketing more important than ever. Changes due to employee attrition, new business models or expansion can open up opportunities for bookkeepers at any moment. Ongoing and consistent targeted marketing ensures you are highly visible to business owners and ready to provide services. They know how and where to reach you.

Need ideas to help you get started? Visit purebookkeeping.com/the-successful-bookkeeper to get access to valuable free resources to jumpstart your marketing and attract new great clients.

MISTAKE #4—GETTING PAID ON INVOICE

No one wants to become a bank for business owners. A bookkeeper should never be in this position. Yet this is exactly what happens to bookkeepers who provide all their work up front and wait for payment. Invoices are sent out and the waiting game begins. It's essential to take steps to avoid this pitfall.

Discussing payment can be uncomfortable for many bookkeepers. Conversations around deposits are avoided and bookkeepers hope everything will run smoothly over the course of their assignment and they will be paid on time. Communicating your expectations up front around payment is crucial. Doing so ensures you are never out of pocket or having to chase down your client. Most bookkeepers discover once a system is set up where money is exchanged prior to work commencing, every aspect of the business relationship improves. The client now has a vested interest in seeing results and the bookkeeper is motivated to deliver. Receiving payment in stages just makes good business sense.

The mantra "money first, pay your staff then pay yourself" is still the best one to follow.

MISTAKE #5—NO ADDITIONAL INCOME STREAMS

Every bookkeeper needs an additional item to sell other than services, a tangible product that benefits clients and generates a passive income. These value-driven items may include resources such as business condition reports. For example, a close friend of mine who is a restaurateur had a bookkeeper who specialized in the Toronto food and beverage sector. She had access to reports which provided invaluable benchmarks and milestone achievements against which she could measure performance. Her bookkeeper was able to capitalize on her prior experience and thus the information provided was extremely valuable. The key idea is these tangible items are desirable because they save your customers time and money. Too often, bookkeepers are giving this information away free and not highlighting the value it delivers.

What product will you provide to differentiate YOUR bookkeeping services? A good place to start is by asking a simple question —if I were in my client's shoes, what resources would benefit me? Strive to be innovative as you brainstorm. What can you provide to showcase your professional expertise? Find something that excites you —something you can't wait to share. Try to be creative in how you package your items too. Package A, B and C should provide different options and qualifications to meet the needs of your diverse client base. Ideally, every bookkeeper should be billing about 10% of their annual income from additional revenue streams.

MISTAKE #6—NOT CHARGING FOR RESCUE JOBS UP FRONT

When a client comes to a bookkeeper in financial distress pleading for help, most bookkeepers jump in and begin the work without charging up front. Also, because the client's desperate state creates a sense of urgency, many bookkeepers will work harder and faster to get their clients back on track. The problem however is rescue jobs carry high risk. There's no guarantee the client can pay for the work at the end. Debbie shares her personal story of losing $4,000 to a rescue job because the client simply couldn't pay. Logically speaking, if business owners can't pay staff or even themselves, they likely can't pay a bookkeeper either! Promises to pay later or once the problems are fixed, are not met. Given the fact rescue jobs require more work and expertise under a tighter timeline, they should always be paid up front. Always maintain the mindset of VALUE as you approach a rescue job. YOU are the lifeblood of that business at that moment and should charge and set payment terms accordingly. If they can't pay, walk away.

MISTAKE #7—NOT GETTING IN FRONT OF ACCOUNTANTS

Accountants are a mainstay for building your bookkeeping business. Since accountants recommend bookkeepers to their clients, it's important to leverage this win-win scenario and begin building relationships. Accountants are advisers to business owners and are the first to see when they may need the services of a bookkeeper. A recommendation from an accountant is a very strong lead. They typically have a high conversion to becoming paid clients.

In our Seven Secrets of Growing Your Bookkeeping Business seminar, we cover much more ground on this important aspect of building your business. Many bookkeepers have benefitted from Debbie's highly effective process for working around issues with accountants and securing more business. The key is to get in front of accountants and present to them why you are a great choice to refer business. Not every accountant will refer business right away, but when you get and stay on her radar you are increasing your odds of getting leads from many accountants.

MISTAKE #8—NO WEBSITE OR THE WEBSITE LACKS THE FUNDAMENTALS

Since working with Peter and Debbie in 2010, I'm still astounded to discover how many bookkeepers don't have a website or it lacks the basic information required to convert a visitor to a lead. In today's business world, having a website is non-negotiable. You MUST have one for practical reasons of accessibility, but also for personal branding which should reflect your personality (About page plus personal photo) and social media marketing (LinkedIn, Facebook, etc.). A website goes beyond describing your bookkeeping services; it is an online presence designed to promote you as likable, approachable, and trustworthy so others will want to do business with you. Keep in mind, it is human nature to want to do business with those we know we can work with. A website that is up-to-date and contains a blog or other interactive discussion board sends the message your business is current and forward thinking. Your business must deliver on all of the above to grow and a strong website is your key to communicating these ideas.

MISTAKE #9—NO SYSTEMS

Michael E. Gerber said it best–creating repeatable, scalable systems is the only way you will ever run a successful business. It's simply not possible to have poor systems and successfully realize the potential of your business. Whether you're building a career as a successful solo practitioner or looking to grow a saleable bookkeeping business, earning $100,000 plus will only happen if your systems are rock solid. The problem, however, is many bookkeepers' systems are only tested after they bring a team of bookkeepers on board. Problems arise early on as team members are unclear about expectations and deliverables. When leadership is weak and benchmarks for success unclear, there are widespread implications around employee satisfaction. Without systems, problems become magnified and businesses quickly go from bad to worse. Moreover, the business owner is once again faced with the time-consuming task of hiring and training. Everyone, including the business owner, must know at all times what to do, how to do it and when they are successful. Excellent systems not only improve quality of output, but productivity and speed as well. This can only lead to greater profits.

MISTAKE #10—NO EXIT PLAN

"Start with the end in mind."

-Stephen R. Covey, *Seven Habits of Highly Effective People: Powerful Lessons in Personal Change*

What do you *really* want to achieve? Do you really want to just work for yourself and make enough money to equal a paid job? Many bookkeepers are focused on the day-to-day without giving much thought to their future retirement. I encourage you to look ahead twenty or thirty years and visualize your retirement package. Where will you be? Will you get that big cheque at the end?

Your bookkeeping business could be an explosive one that you build into a profitable operation. This is NOT fantasy. This happens all the time. I have personally met bookkeepers who have built highly saleable businesses worth $500,000 plus with an eye on retiring very comfortably. You may be wondering, who actually buys a bookkeeping business? Accountants do and so do other bookkeepers that want to expand their business quickly. Successful bookkeeping businesses (based on excellent systems) are a cash cow opportunity. When you build a business that runs itself and has predictable revenue, you have an asset that can be sold. I would say this is the ultimate reward. You make a great living during your career building a profitable business then sell it to really enjoy your retirement as a successful bookkeeper.

FINAL THOUGHTS

Take a moment to check in with yourself. Do you feel confident and ready to move forward with your next steps? Are there changes you would like to implement right now? The key point I want to stress is you have everything you need right now to be successful and grow your business while avoiding common pitfalls along the way. My dream and business vision for you as a bookkeeper is to be so highly valued your clients can't wait to work with you. You are their go-to person not only for financial reports but also for uncovering that strategic edge that will help their business excel. Trust that business owners will look at you this way if you have a mindset that is grounded in value and self-worth.

Looking ahead, the final chapter will focus on action plans to help you avoid mistakes and do things right the first time. This all begins when your end goals are in clear sight.

CHAPTER 9

THE 10 PILLARS OF BUSINESS

"If you don't have time to do it right you must have time to do it over."

-Anonymous

We've covered a lot of ground so far…

You've now arrived at a critical turning point and have a big decision to make. Will you take those first steps towards the future you desire? My sincere hope is you are feeling motivated and ready to jump in. You're ready to join a dynamic global community of *great* bookkeepers who are changing the world. Everything you need to succeed is within your grasp. With this in mind, we'll now turn our attention to what I refer to as the "pillars" or domains of business, the foundation on which your successful bookkeeping business will be built.

Growing a business is complex. It's easy to get off track and feel discouraged. As a business coach, I have found the best strategy for thinking about how a business will grow begins with identifying the different components and how they fit together. These will be explored in detail in this chapter. This easy-to-follow framework provides a clear and objective approach to business planning and analysis. *What do I mean by business pillars?* This idea was first introduced to me by Peter Cook, business coach extraordinaire, who helped Debbie build her profitable bookkeeping business. Early on, in order for Debbie to thrive in each domain or pillar of her business, from leadership and finances to marketing and services, she had to be not only 100% committed, but LOVE every part of her business —the past, present and future.

In his publication *Love Your Business: The Method,* Peter aims to help businesses develop an "authentic thriving mindset and culture." Peter's business philosophy focuses on the concept of "the more we love, the more we thrive." Business owners who fully embrace the 10 key business domains will experience the most success and satisfaction. There are key activities you MUST do so you will love your business and, in turn, ensure others love it too. This includes your customers, employers, stakeholders or anyone who is associated with your business. Everyone must have a genuine interest in your business success to make it all work.

I encourage you to give careful attention to each pillar of business during your creative phase. Doing so will ensure you effectively grow your bookkeeping business.

LEADERSHIP

Be a Visionary:

Your leadership role should go beyond being the most powerful decision-maker in your business. Providing inspiration and finding ways to unite your team means communicating your Vision, Mission and Values within your organization. You are the driver of your business. You breathe life into it.

Be a Creator:

As business owner, you give birth to your business entity. There are parallels to be drawn with becoming a parent. When you decide to have a child, you take responsibility for raising that child and steering him or her towards success. Your child becomes an individual with a distinct personality.

Excel at Communication:

Where are you going and what do you want your business to be? Communicating your past (where you've come from) and where you're going (your future) are part of your business story that YOU must communicate. Place importance on defining your story and articulating it to others. Believe in it with all your heart!

Motivate Others:

A great leader is one who motivates others to take ownership of their work. Your bookkeeping team will only feel successful and motivated to produce top results if they are valued. Celebrate successes as your business grows. Job satisfaction comes down to how valued people feel.

Be a Trail Blazer:

Leadership is about harnessing your entrepreneurial spirit to drive your business forward. A leader will find innovative ways to network and uncover new opportunities, working at full speed during the sole creator phase.

MANAGEMENT

Be Accountable:

The best way to ensure your staff is accountable is to begin with yourself. Take ownership and set an example at all times. Be certain the business vision and ideas you put forth become *more* than words. Delivering results is crucial.

Plan for Success:

As a bookkeeping business owner and manager, you have a unique responsibility for both generating business ideas and implementing them. Remember, YOU are sailing the ship—no one else. Review SMART goal setting as you plan.

Establish Measures:

The best habit you can develop as a business manager is introducing measures for business success. Employees should know what measures are in place to gauge their performance. What measures will be applied to bookkeeping projects so that results can be assessed?

Manage with Integrity:

Purposeful decision-making combined with a winning and positive attitude ensures your team believes in the goals you have set. Priorities you have identified will be understood and respected.

Be an Agent for Change:

Starting a business is about preparing for a great adventure. With this in mind, expect twists and turns along your journey and adapt your strategy as needed. Change means growth. Be a champion of change so you can rally your staff to embrace change too.

PEOPLE

Team Building:

What types of people are best suited to your business? Effective bookkeeping teams are comprised of bookkeepers who have "how to" skills as well as soft skills. For example, they deliver detail-oriented, accurate results and communicate them professionally and with ease. A "can-do" attitude is essential.

Hiring:

Having a system for hiring is important. What approach to recruiting will ensure the candidate knows how to do the job? How will you know if they'll stay the course? (A "skills test" forms part of the Pure Bookkeeping Recruitment Module to measure practical bookkeeping skills. Other questions are aimed at uncovering a candidate's values and personal qualities.)

Training:

What do you want your bookkeepers to do and why? HOW specifically should they do their job? Training is your opportunity to set your team on a track for success. Establish training that is aimed at delivering strong results. Importantly, training increases consistent quality output.

Employee Retention:

Hiring and training is an investment of time and energy. With this in mind, make job satisfaction a top priority. Create systems that measure success! How will your staff know they are successful? Jobs that have clear parameters—a beginning and an end—are the most satisfying.

Communication:

Problems arise in business when communication is weak. Focus your attention on business-related communication issues rather than personal ones. Beware of using email as your go-to communication method for resolving issues.

FINANCES

Clarity First:

Do you understand the numbers? Where are you now? What are your short and long-term projections? At all times, know where your business is at. Get the help you need. *Being relaxed around your finances takes you out of survival mode and engages the creative parts of your brain.*

Understanding the Plan:

A key part of growing your business is understanding benchmarks and standards for your industry. What are the *true* costs of operating your bookkeeping business? Consider overhead and fixed costs such as bookkeeping software, licenses, office furniture, leases, hiring and more.

Knowing the Targets:

Make sure you are always working towards well-defined goals. Are they realistic? Is your team set up for success? Revisit SMART goals for a comprehensive guide to goal setting.

Your Plan B:

If you're not reaching your goals, why not? What needs to change? Having a flexible approach to running your business will help you adapt to new threats and opportunities. Running into obstacles is to be expected. What's important is getting back on your feet.

Keeping the Books:

Don't be shy about hiring a bookkeeper to keep the books for your business! There's a good chance your books are not impeccable. You're not alone. Have you ever heard the phrase "a plumbers taps always leaks"? Give yourself a break. Just because you are an expert, this is not enough reason to take it on. In fact, hiring another bookkeeper may help you be more objective and less emotional about numbers.

SYSTEMS

Commit to Continuous Improvement:

Once you've developed your systems for every part of your business, commit to making them even better! The Japanese word *kaizen*, "improvement", refers to the philosophy of committing to continuous improvement in all pillars of business. Involve all team members. Also encourage your team to offer suggestions and help your business become even better.

Document Everything:

Fix problems and document how you fixed them. Take notes and document procedures to establish streamlined approaches to operating your business. When Debbie first began documenting her business, this formed the foundation for Pure Bookkeeping today—3,000 pages of systems and documents created over a decade.

Tip: Keeping records may seem like a lot of work. Try starting with one page and build your systems from there. Being consistent will save you time in the long run. *Pure Bookkeeping could only have started this way!*

Leverage your Expertise:

I can't stress enough the importance of using systems as leverage to grow your bookkeeping business. Keep in mind Michael Gerber's mantra "repeatable, scalable" as you discover shortcuts and best practices to save you time and make you money.

Implement your Systems:

If you've expended the effort to document everything and create your systems, make sure everyone (including you) uses them. Set an example by following protocol and provide feedback when staff doesn't adhere to systems.

Test your Systems:

Testing plays a large role in continuous improvement. As you implement new systems, observe what works and what doesn't. Look for ways to become more efficient. For example, are there too many administrative tasks to support your method of invoicing? Would online project management facilitate faster communication?

INTERNET

Inside your Business:

Email is only one of many ways to communicate online with your team. Make full use of the Internet and explore how you can streamline your communication around key projects by using virtual shared spaces and project management programs.

Outside your Business:

Today's wide range of powerful virtual tools such as cloud storage and delivery means every part of your business can become easier, faster and better. Gain a competitive edge by offering your clients innovative services via the Internet, such as downloading reports. What works best for them?

Your Markets:

What's the best way to reach your ideal customers online? Should you design an email campaign or create a targeted ad on social media? Even today, the potential of the Internet is largely untapped by businesses. Ask yourself what you can do differently to gain market share.

Your Online Tools:

Your business website is still your single best online tool. When your prospects are shopping for a bookkeeper, make sure they can find you. At a glance, your website should communicate a) who you are and why you're the best, b) your services and areas of expertise, and c) how to reach you.

Tip: Make the most of your website traffic by encouraging visitors to sign up for your bookkeeping newsletter or blog posts. This is one of the easiest passive ways to build your customer database. As a plus, you will be their first choice for future bookkeeping services.

Adapt to New Technology:

Part of your commitment to continuous improvement is keeping up to date with new technologies that benefit you and your customers. Be open to learning, training and expanding your horizons. Are there new ways you can incorporate technology to attract tech-savvy customers?

PRODUCTS & SERVICES

Create Value:

If you are committed to creating products and services that people will LOVE, your business will thrive. Creating value begins with loving every part of your business and letting that passion shine through. Know the tremendous value your bookkeeping business offers the small business owner, namely peace of mind, decreased stress, greater freedom, and so much more.

Be Innovative:

How can you do business differently? The bookkeeping industry is entrenched with old ideas. Carve out new ways to provide better services for your clients. Will your customers bring ideas to the table? Some of the best innovations result from customer feedback.

Differentiate Yourself:

Bookkeeping is a competitive business. What is your unique value proposition? Differentiating yourself so your bookkeeping services stand out may be the biggest challenge you face. Think of creative ways you might package your services and create a saleable item that provides additional revenue.

Seek Feedback:

The best way to determine how to improve your products and services is to ask your customers. Gather information in any way you can —surveys, phone calls, or during face-to-face meetings at tradeshows and networking events. Be specific about the information you are seeking.

Make Improvements:

Be sure to put great customer feedback to good use; continue to develop and refine your products and services. Also be sure to let your customers know you've listened and fulfilled their wish lists. Your integrity and enthusiasm will build long-term loyalty.

MARKETING

Know Your Story:

Once you are committed to your Mission Statement and Vision, share it with everyone! Practice your "elevator speech" so you can explain what your business is about in 20 seconds or less. Get comfortable introducing your business to others using words that are natural and sincere rather than sales-focused.

Own Your Story:

Live and breathe the story you've created. Love the story of your business journey and how you arrived at the point you are today. Everyone enjoys hearing a good business story. Yours will be remembered if you share it with enthusiasm.

Know Your Customers:

Do you know who your ideal customer is? What services do they need and what industries do they represent? For example, our Pure Bookkeeping customers are bookkeepers who want to build a highly successful bookkeeping practice or business. Our customers do NOT include bookkeepers about to retire.

Create a Message:

Create a powerful marketing message (value proposition) that resonates with your markets. The message must speak directly to your customers' needs, expressing specifically the value your bookkeeping business offers. For more help, download the *Pure Bookkeeping 7X5 Marketing Plan* from the Pure Bookkeeping website.

Be a Networker:

Seek out opportunities for professional networking and connect with as many prospects as you can. Encourage others to refer your services and always carry business cards. A key part of networking is following up on questions about your business services and rates.

SALES

Pricing:

How will you price your products and services? Will you package your services? Many new businesses test prices early on and make adjustments. Let value drive your pricing and start as high as you can; it's easier to adjust prices lower, if necessary, later on.

Sales Management:

Measuring your success comes down to knowing the benchmarks for success as determined by your financial projections and goals. If you are managing a team who handle multiple projects, have a system for reporting and measuring milestone achievements.

Selling:

Get comfortable selling the products and services your bookkeeping business offers by knowing your sales "pitch" and fee ranges. Know your sales process. Is there a designated team member who handles invoicing? Who answers questions about prices?

Adjusting Prices:

Occasionally you will have to communicate price increases to customers. Giving yourself a raise is important. Keep in mind customers who select your services on price alone will leave you regardless for a cheaper rate. Always sell on value.

Negotiation:

Become an expert negotiator in all your sales transactions. If it seems reasonable to adjust a bookkeeping project fee, be sure it makes good business sense. Be assertive and do not give into being pressured or rushed.

SERVICE

Be the Best:

Commit to excellence in service and communicate the importance of service to your team. Be as specific as possible. What does excellent service mean to your customers? How can your service offer a competitive edge?

Train your Staff:

Take pro-active steps to ensure your excellent service is put into action! Train staff on your service expectations, such as the importance of returning phone calls and emails within 24 hours or responding swiftly to quality concerns. Any service issue that's important to YOU must be shared with staff.

Implement a System:

Documenting how you resolve customer service issues are a great habit and well worth your time. Take every obstacle you face as a learning opportunity so you can easily handle similar problems down the road. As steps and solutions become a system, your team will be able to respond faster and more efficiently.

Communicate Well:

> Most service problems in business arise due to poor communication. Expectations are not made clear or key information is not relayed to customers. As a business owner, you need to give thought to the best ways to communicate to eliminate misunderstandings. Sometimes the solution is as simple as creating a project checklist.

Be a Model:

> Do you "walk the talk"? Raise the bar on service expectations by setting an example for others to follow. Ensure all your communications reflect a positive and winning tone and put the customer first. Focus on win-win solutions.

MOVING FORWARD

Keep the pillars of your business in the forefront of your mind as you move into the next phase of your journey, creating a Successful Bookkeeper Action Plan. Use this chapter as a reference and check in regularly to see what pillars you need to work on.

Importantly, push yourself to become proficient in those areas of your business that are weakest or present the greatest challenge. Be mindful of spending too much time doing the tasks where you have the greatest level of comfort. Pushing yourself out of your comfort zone involves embracing all opportunities for learning along the way.

You may discover some areas we've discussed require more work than others, especially if you find yourself in unfamiliar waters. For example, if you are a customer service-oriented bookkeeper, committing to excellence and setting high expectations will likely come naturally. If you're more technically oriented or introverted, sales management and negotiation may be your biggest test.

Remember each pillar is equally important and forms the foundation of your business. When each pillar is rock solid, you will have something built to last. Love every part of your bookkeeping business and I guarantee you will create something truly amazing!

CHAPTER 10

OUTLINE: THE SUCCESSFUL BOOKKEEPER ACTION PLAN

"If you don't design your own life plan, chances are you'll fall into someone else's plan. And guess what they've planned for you? Not much."

-Jim Rohn

The main goal of this book has been to provide a solid foundation on which you can begin to build a successful business, in whatever way *you* define success. Only with all the pieces of the puzzle laid out before you can you begin to see how your business and life can take shape. Throughout this process, I've encouraged you to think through some key questions —what are my barriers to achieving my goals? Do I want to become a successful sole practitioner or a successful business owner? We also discussed the two most important building blocks of accomplishment—mindset and commitment. Every victory you will ever achieve must be built on this foundation. You are the visionary for your business and only you have the power to move from dreaming to creating.

You might be wondering…what's next? This chapter is about putting it all together. Now is the time to bring everything covered so far in the book into sharper focus. With your mind now set on achieving your goals and greater awareness of the Pillars of Business you need to pay attention to, you need an Action Plan. With this in mind, this chapter presents a more interactive workbook format. As you move into the action planning stage, I will recap key points introduced so far along with some practical exercises to help you get started.

TAKING YOUR FIRST STEPS

Creating your Action Plan is about committing to a future you envision and desire. Are you ready and committed to getting started? When the time is right, find a quiet space where you can work comfortably without distractions. Getting into the right "head space" is important too. Clear your schedule to take all the time you need to think creatively and plan. Remember to relax and open your mind. It is common to "fear the unknown" and hesitate when moving from the intangible to something real. Trust? you are building something great!

Keep the big picture in mind. What is this journey *really* about? What positive changes will happen in your life now and in the near future as you work through your Action Plan? Remember, success and happiness don't happen by chance; they are the result of a perfect storm involving taking risks, believing and persevering. At this moment, you are embarking on what just might be the most exciting journey of your life! Stay committed, feel the momentum and trust that opportunities and resources will be there. My task will be to break down your Action Planning into simple and easy to digest steps.

Let's get started...

ACTION PLAN SUMMARY

STEP 1. ASSESS YOUR MINDSET

Where do you want to go? Do you really want to take this journey? Since having the right mindset is crucial to achieving your business goals, assessing where you are right now marks an important first step in your Action Plan. The points, map and compass alone are not enough to reach your goals. The best tools in the business will only work when you're ready to commit.

In Chapter 4 *Where do you want to go?*, we discussed how each of us perceives ourselves through our own filters. Our filters are unique and reinforce the beliefs we hold at a subconscious level. "I am just a book-keeper" or "I don't know how to be an entrepreneur" may be some of the self-perceptions you have.

The following exercises are designed to help you (a) better understand your mindset at this moment and (b) better understand your core values that are driving your business decisions right now.

Exercise A. Understanding the Power of Vision

Everything we see around us was first created in the mind. In other words, reality is created by our thoughts. Look at your life today. What are 5 things you have achieved you once thought were impossible? List them in Column 1. Next, what actions did you take to make them happen?

Achievements	Action/Steps Taken
1.	
2.	
3.	
4.	
5.	

Reflect on your mindset at the time you took action. Think about how your mindset empowered you to reach these goals.

Exercise B: Understanding your core values

Why do I want a successful bookkeeping business? Your core values, or fundamental beliefs, underlie every decision you make in your life. They are the essence of who you are and steer you in the right direction. Your decision to go on this business journey must be aligned with the values you subscribe to.

Think of 5 experiences in your life that made you happy. List them in Column 1. Now try to recall what it was about these experiences that brought you happiness. Next, try to identify the Core Values that relate to these moments of happiness.

Experience	How did this experience create happiness?	Core Value
Example: Completing Bookkeeping Certification	-personal sense of accomplishment -proud to finish despite obstacles along the way -pride in taking charge of my future/having a vision	Integrity
1.		
2.		
3.		
4.		
5.		

STEP 2. ASSESS YOUR COMMITMENT

How committed are you to the bookkeeping business you are planning? In Chapter 5 "Committing to your Mission", we explored the idea that commitment really comes down to a personal decision. You must make a decision to commit to the future you want. Commitment is a powerful mindset that is at the heart of your business success. Your personal path for success must be grounded in 100% commitment.

Exercise A: Commitment Scale

Put your commitment to action to the test. Below is a scale that shows Commitment on a scale of 1-10 (10=highest).

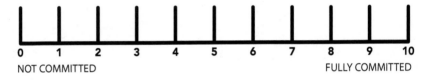

```
0    1    2    3    4    5    6    7    8    9    10
NOT COMMITTED                              FULLY COMMITTED
```

My commitment level at this moment is _____

If you are not a 10, ask yourself why. Is there something holding you back from being totally committed? Recall that fear and commitment are two different things. The space between where you are now and full commitment often comes down to fear. You may be feeling uncertain you can achieve your goals. This is NOT the same as not being committed.

Fears around failure or uncertainty about how you will achieve your business goals can cloud your judgement around your ability to understand how committed you truly are.

Exercise B: Commitment Statement

Self-limiting beliefs are barriers to your success. By identifying self-limiting beliefs, you can begin to be objective and change your self-definition. The purpose of this exercise is to (a) understand what self-limiting beliefs and fears are getting in your way of commitment and (b) find a strategy to tackle them by creating a Commitment Statement.

Step 1. What Self-Limiting beliefs do you have (about yourself, your abilities, or circumstances) that are preventing you from fully committing to growing your business? List them in Column 1.

Step 2. For each of belief, create a Contrast Statement to negate it. Place in Column 2.

Step 3. Next, create a Commitment Statement. This should be an action-oriented step to help you change your mindset and reinforce your commitment.

Self-limiting Belief (Negative)	Contrast Statement (Positive)	Commitment Statement
Example: I don't have time to reach my goal (secure 3 new clients this month)	I have 1 hour a week to work on my goal	I will work 1 hour per week to reach my goal by organizing an email and phone campaign to introduce my bookkeeping services to local businesses

Self-limiting Belief (Negative)	Contrast Statement (Positive)	Commitment Statement

STEP 3. CREATE YOUR MISSION STATEMENT

What is YOUR reason for existence? Similar to a personal statement, a business Mission Statement originates from understanding your business purpose and how it relates to the goals you have.

EXERCISE A: DEVELOP YOUR MISSION STATEMENT

A good Mission Statement answers a need(s). Your customers will experience "pain" in their businesses and your bookkeeping services will be the answer. Your business will fit somewhere in the spectrum.

What does your customer need from you? The best place to understand what specific needs your business will meet is to understand the gap between where your customers are now (Point A) and where they want to be (Point B). Your business will move your customers from Point A to Point B. The question of HOW this will be done is the key message articulated by your Mission Statement. See visual below:

Try to understand the crux of what business owners need. Try to put yourself in their shoes and imagine what scenarios or situations create stress. How does anxiety impact the business owner, employees and the community? Also, consider how your services fit in. How will you remedy their pain? Create a list below:

Point A–Current State What does stress look like for your customer?	Point B–Desired State What does Stress-Free look like for your customer?
Example: not being able to pay employees	Cash flow for the next 90 Days has been mapped out to cover all expenses and any gap has been identified.

Notice everything you list in Column 2 (Stress-Free) relates to financial success, more free time and less working hours. Now indicate how your bookkeeping services will help move your customer from Point A to Point B.

Exercise B: Refine Your Mission Statement

Your Mission Statement speaks directly to your VALUE proposition. The words you choose should instantly connect with your customers.

Consider Debbie's mission statement: "We love to empower business owners around their finances by removing confusion, fear and uncertainty and replacing it with clarity, freedom and control."

Both resonate strongly with customers. In these statements lie the promise of better financial security and peace of mind. Based on your list of what defines Stress-Free for your customer, describe how your business helps reach that goal. Create 5 statements. Is there a special area of expertise that should be noted in your Mission Statement? For example: "Our efficient and accurate payroll services give business owners peace of mind."

STEP 4. ESTABLISH SMART GOALS

In Chapter 6, we discussed the key difference between working towards specific SMART goals and simply working hard. Getting specific about your goals, the steps you need to take to reach them, significantly increases the likelihood you'll take your business in the right direction. With your Mission Statement established, you are now ready to set goals.

Recall that SMART is an acronym for a 5 step method which outlines the criteria to set goals. The idea is to align objectives and action plans. Goals must be Specific, Measurable, Attainable/Assignable, Relevant/Realistic and Time-based.

Your Mission Statement _____

_____

_____

Exercise A: Creating and Testing Your SMART Goals

You now have a better understanding of your Core Values and what's important to you. Now you can begin thinking about your business goals and how they are an expression of these values. What business goals do you want to reach?

Start by creating one Goal Statement that describes *as specifically as possible* what you want to achieve by growing your bookkeeping business. Writing out the goal as a statement will help you express it simply and as straightforward as possible.

Example: "I want to grow my bookkeeping business by 25% this year."

Your Goal Statement _____

_____

Specific

Can your goal be stated in one sentence? A specific goal means you can easily answer all "W" questions such as Who, What, Where, When, Which, Where and Why. For example, what do I want to achieve and when?

Measurable

How much? How many? How will I know I'm on the right track? A measurable goal means you know exactly where you are at any time on your path.

Attainable/Assignable

Is your goal one that can be achieved given your current life situation and mindset? Can it be accomplished?

Relevant/Realistic

Does your goal reflect your larger life goals? Is this the right time? Is it worthwhile and desirable?

Time-based

Is there a timeframe and deadline for your goal? What will you do today? How about one month from now?

Exercise B: Turning Goals into Action

When you feel confident your Goal Statement meets the SMART criteria, begin brainstorming around your goals. How specifically will you meet them? A good technique is to break down your goal into smaller more manageable goals. In other words, you must now create a subset of goals which, when achieved, bring you closer to the goals expressed in your Goal Statement.

A practical technique is to imagine you have already achieved your goal. Vision your success by turning your Goal Statement into past tense: i.e. "I grew my bookkeeping business by 25% this year."

What specific steps did you take to reach your goal? Focus on core activities rather than details.

Achieved Goal"	Activities to Support Goal
Grew by 25% this year	I joined a networking group and contacted 20 new prospects.
	I launched a bookkeeping newsletter
	I hired two bookkeepers
	I upgraded my skills to expand my services

STEP 5. APPLY A SWOT ANALYSIS (STRENGTHS/WEAKNESSES/OPPORTUNI-TIES/THREATS)

You have created your Statement Goal and you are clear on your objectives. Now you are ready to do a SWOT Analysis to identify internal and external factors that will be either favourable or unfavourable to achieving your business goal.

A SWOT analysis of your bookkeeping business is a key part of your Action Plan. A strategic review of your business will enable you to take advantage of both current marketplace opportunities and future ones.

Exercise 1: SWOT Analysis

A SWOT (or SWOT matrix) is a structured planning method used to evaluate the strengths, weaknesses, opportunities and threats involved in a project or in a business. A SWOT analysis used for a product, place, industry or person.

Below is an example:

	FAVORABLE	UNFAVORABLE
INTERNAL	**STRENGTH** 1. What are your strengths? 2. What do you do better than others? 3. What unique capabilities and resources do you possess? 4. What do others perceive as your strengths?	**WEAKNESSES** 1. What are your weaknesses? 2. What do your competitors do better than you? 3. What can you improve given the current situation? 4. What do others perceive as your weaknesses?
EXTERNAL	**OPPORTUNITIES** 1. What trends or conditions may positively impact you? 2. What opportunities are available to you?	**THREATS** 1. What trends or conditions may negatively impact you? 2. What are your competitors doing that may impact you? 3. Do you have solid financial support? 4. What impact do your weaknesses have on the threats to you?

Exercise A: Fill out your own Business SWOT below.

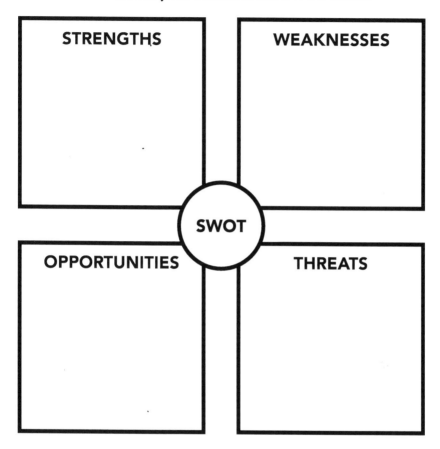

Exercise B: Understanding Your Business SWOT

- Once you finish the SWOT analysis, you have identified some important issues you can focus on in your business to move forward. Take time to review the results and form a plan by:

- Knowing your strengths and making a list of ways you can make them even stronger

- Brainstorming ways you can minimize your weaknesses
- Creating measurable goals for each of the opportunities you identified
- Figuring out how you can use your strengths to decrease the threats

The SWOT analysis data will give you a big-picture perspective to start your strategic planning process. If you're ready, use it as a stepping stone to a larger process that will help transform your business.

STEP 6. THINKING WITH THE END IN MIND

In Chapter 8, "10 Mistakes Bookkeepers Make", we explored the key 10 problem areas that present obstacles to bookkeepers while growing their businesses. In most cases, problems arise when bookkeeping systems are poorly implemented or simply don't exist. The best way to avoid making these all-too-common mistakes is to take a pro-active approach now in the Action Planning stages:

EXERCISE A: PRO-ACTIVE GOAL SETTING

For each of the 10 Mistakes in Column 1, create a Positive Goal statement that counters the mistake. See the example below.

10 Mistakes Bookkeepers Make	Positive Goal Statement
Bookkeepers don't charge enough money	Example: I will charge in the top 25% of my market place. My pricing will reflect the value I deliver. I will send out a letter by X date to past customers of a price increase and incorporate this pricing into my new client presentations.

10 Mistakes Bookkeepers Make	Positive Goal Statement
Bookkeepers think that building a book-keeping business is about doing the books	
Bookkeepers don't do any marketing	
Bookkeepers get paid on invoice	
Bookkeepers don't have an additional income stream	
Bookkeepers don't charge for rescue jobs upfront	
Bookkeepers don't get in front of accountants	
Bookkeepers don't have websites	
Bookkeepers have inefficient systems	
Bookkeepers have no exit plan	

Exercise B: Turning Positive Goals into Action

Now take your Positive Goal Statements and brainstorm the pro-active actions you can take to achieve your goal. See the example below.

10 Positive Goal Statements	Action(s) to Take to Achieve Goal
Example: I will charge enough money	Example: I will implement a price structure that reflects the value of my services

STEP 7. ASSESSING THE 10 PILLARS OF BUSINESS

Rank each of the 10 Pillars on a scale (i.e. What Pillar needs the most attention/work?).

STEP 8. IMPLEMENTING THE 10 PILLARS OF BUSINESS

The following questions are associated with the 10 Pillars of Business discussed in Chapter 9. Go through and answers the ones that are obvious to you now. Come back later and spend more time on the ones that challenge you. This is not about getting it right, but rather stimulating your creative thinking for your business.

LEADERSHIP		
10 Pillars	**The Challenge**	**Answer (be specific)**
Be a Visionary	How specifically will you communicate your Mission and Values to your team?	
Be a Creator	How will you ensure you are continually creating in your business?	
Excel at Communication	How will you measure your ability to communicate?	
Motivate Others	How will you measure how well you motivate others?	
Be a Trail Blazer	What can you do to inspire your entrepreneurial spirit?	

MANAGEMENT		
10 Pillars	**The Challenge**	**Answer (be specific)**
Be Accountable	How specifically will you hold yourself and others accountable?	
Plan for Success	When and how often will you make time to plan for your business?	
Establish Measures	How will you create measures in your business?	
Manage with Integrity	How will you know if you are maintaining integrity in your business?	
Be an Agent for Change	What will you do to measure your capacity for change?	

PEOPLE		
10 Pillars	**The Challenge**	**Answer (be specific)**
Team Building	What makes a right fit for a person to work within your business?	
Hiring	How will you assess the right fit for hiring team members?	
Training	How will you train your team and validate they are trained?	

Employee Retention	How will your team know they are thriving in your business?	
Communication	What can you do to create an environment of open and respectful communication?	

FINANCE

10 Pillars	The Challenge	Answer (be specific)
Clarity First	What can you do to bring clarity to your finances?	
Understanding the Plan	Do you have a plan to get your business to a desired financial position?	
Knowing the Targets	Is your team aligned with your plan and working to move your business forward?	
Your Plan B	What is the back up plan to your plan?	
Keeping the Books	Are your books as impeccable as your client's books?	

SYSTEMS

10 Pillars	The Challenge	Answer (be specific)
Commit to Continuous Improvement	What systems does your business need?	
Document Everything	How can you and your staff begin to document everything?	
Leverage your Expertise	How are you unpacking your experiences and expectations from your head and into a procedures document?	
Implement your Systems	What can you do to get yourself and team working from a system?	
Test your Systems	When will you take time to evaluate your systems and plan improvement?	

INTERNET		
10 Pillars	**The Challenge**	**Answer (be specific)**
Inside your Business	Where inside your business can you leverage more of the internet?	
Outside your Business	Where outside your business can you leverage more of the internet?	
10 Pillars	**The Challenge**	**Answer (be specific)**
Your Markets	What ways can you leverage the internet to reach your market?	
Your Online Tools	What online tools could improve the way you do business?	
Adapt to New Technology	What can you do to learn more about up and coming technologies to stay ahead of the curve?	
PRODUCTS & SERVICES		
10 Pillars	**The Challenge**	**Answer (be specific)**
Create Value	Is your business creating value? How can you measure and optimize the value you deliver?	
Be Innovative	What can you do differently in your business that would provide more value or create efficiencies?	
Differentiate Yourself	What is your unique value proposition?	
Seek Feedback	How can you get feedback about you and your business?	
Make Improvements	What improvements can you make now?	

MARKETING		
10 Pillars	**The Challenge**	**Answer (be specific)**
Know Your Story	What is your elevator speech?	
Own Your Story	How can you bring more of your story to your business?	
Know Your Customers	How can you get to know your customers better?	
Create a Message	Where can you share your business message?	
Be a Networker	Where and when can you get in front of more people and prospects?	

SALES		
10 Pillars	**The Challenge**	**Answer (be specific)**
Pricing	Is your pricing aligned with the value you deliver?	
Sales Management	What metrics can you set up to measure your sales performance?	
Selling	Have you defined your sales process?	
Adjusting Prices	Do you have your response to price objections scripted?	
Negotiation	What levers can you adjust in negotiating with customers?	

SERVICE		
10 Pillars	**The Challenge**	**Answer (be specific)**
Be the Best	How can you measure your service and then improve it?	
Train your Staff	Have you trained your staff in your service standards?	
Implement a System	Do you have a system in place to capture service issues?	

Communicate Well	How can you discover your customer's knowledge and understanding of your business?	
Be a Model	What can you do to improve your personal service to your customers and staff?	

STEP 9. SWOT ANALYSIS OF THE 10 PILLARS OF BUSINESS

You've now stimulated your creativity with the questions for each pillar of your business. Complete a SWOT Analysis on each pillar. As you complete this exercise actions and goals will naturally occur to you. Record those in the next section.

STEP 10. SETTING GOALS FOR THE 10 PILLARS OF BUSINESS

Set a goal for each pillar then create an action plan for each.

In a spreadsheet, you can organize it by using the below headings.

PILLAR I GOAL I ACTIONS I BY WHEN

Scale each pillar and the 5 factors in each.

CHAPTER 11

WHAT'S NEXT

"Whatever you can do, or dream you can do, begin it. Boldness has genius, power, and magic in it. Begin it now."

- William H. Murray, The Story of Everest

What a journey this has been.

Reading this book, you've likely discovered many new and incredibly useful tools you can use to take your bookkeeping business to soaring heights.

You wouldn't have come across that information if you weren't open to learning.

You see, not everyone is like you.

Many bookkeepers just want to be technicians and continue to be invisible.

But, not you.

You're different because you want more for your business and life. You understand there are things you don't know that offer the keys to the success you truly want.

As a result, you're willing to be a ferocious learner to fill the gaps by doing whatever it takes including investing in yourself.

You deserve the business and life you've always wanted and, now, you're doing something about it.

Just by finishing this book, you're already ahead of 90% of the bookkeepers out there.

You've grown and your life and business will be better for it.

So, what's next on your journey?

To truly be a successful bookkeeper that achieves what her heart desires, it doesn't happen by reading one book.

It's a good start, but there's still a long path to go.

You'll need to learn step-by-step to create powerful systems in your business and strengthen your mindset even further, so you can work through challenges and persevere until you receive the outcomes you're looking for.

In the upcoming pages, you'll find terrific resources that will definitely fill the gaps in your education and will give you proven and practical strategies that will help give you the profitable bookkeeping business you've always wanted.

Well, our time together has to come an end.

It's been my incredible honour and pleasure to walk with you on this first step of your exciting path towards becoming a successful bookkeeper.

You will do great things if you have the passion, talent, perseverance, the right mentors and tools at your disposal.

The work you do is extremely important and the people you serve need you now more than ever.

Build a business you love and every day will be a success.

The Pure Bookkeeping System

Based on Debbie Roberts' highly successful 30-year plus bookkeeping experience, Pure Bookkeeping offers a comprehensive easy-to-understand framework for setting up, marketing and growing a highly profitable bookkeeping business. Pure Bookkeeping is a proven and powerful system that empowers bookkeepers to charge top rates and attract the best clients while managing their businesses in a way that affords more free time. Debbie's robust system is the ultimate go-to toolkit for bookkeepers who want to grow their businesses faster, focusing on business execution rather than business design.

Find out MORE at
www.purebookkeeping.com/the-system

Seven Secrets of Growing Your Bookkeeping Business Seminar

Attended by over 3000 bookkeepers (and counting!), the Seven Secrets of Growing Your Bookkeeping Business Seminar is revolutionizing the bookkeeping industry. Since launching in 2010, the "Seven Secrets" seminars and webinars have benefited bookkeepers worldwide by delivering strategies they need to overcome the common concerns around feeling overworked, under-appreciated, under-paid or all three. Bookkeepers who are well qualified, know their software, but simply haven't had the time or opportunity to really understand marketing, HR or business administration will benefit from the valuable insight offered in this highly sought-after seminar.

Find out MORE at
www.purebookkeeping.com/seminars

You've read about the journey of Debbie Roberts who is the The Successful Bookkeeper and her coach Peter Cook. Now read the celebrated book they wrote with Mega Best-Seller Author, Michael E. Gerber *The E-Myth Bookkeeper.*

Running a successful bookkeeping business is a juggling act. You need expertise in your area of bookkeeping to provide services to clients. You also need the know-how to run a small business. You've probably been well prepared by your education and experience for the technical ins and outs of a bookkeeping practice. Yet, what training has prepared you to run a business?

Introducing:
The E-Myth Bookkeeper

Combining the wisdom of renowned business development expert, Michael E. Gerber and the industry expertise of Pure Bookkeeping co-founders, Debbie Roberts and Peter Cook, The E-Myth Bookkeeper fills the knowledge gap in this powerful one-stop guide that is loaded with practical advice you can easily use to take your business to levels you didn't think possible!

From the Best-Selling Author of *The E-Myth*

The **E** Myth

Bookkeeper

Why Most Bookkeeping Practices Don't Work and What to Do About It

MICHAEL E. GERBER
DEBBIE ROBERTS
PETER COOK

The Course

Would you like to build a bookkeeping business to sell?

So many bookkeepers are worried about making day-to-day income that they forget they have an actual asset on their hands.

Small business expert and author of the NY Times Best-Selling book, *The E-Myth Revisited*, Michael E. Gerber will help you break out of that limiting mindset and propel you to new heights with his newest creation, The Course!

He will inspire and teach you a condensed and powerful process to give you the essential steps needed to build your company for sale.

To learn MORE at
www.thesuccessfulbookkeeper.com/gerber

ABOUT THE AUTHOR

Michael Palmer is the CEO of Pure Bookkeeping North America, an author and host of The Successful Bookkeeper podcast.

His inspirational work has had a positive global impact on the bookkeeping industry especially with the hundreds of bookkeepers he's coached to great success.

Before helping the bookkeeping community, Michael had 25 years experience in the business world where he worked with thousands of entrepreneurs and had an extensive background in large corporate environments such as Dun & Bradstreet and Salesforce.com that involved sales, management and project management.

An accomplished communicator and ferocious learner, he also discovered wisdom by speaking with many recognizable thought leaders including New York Times best-selling authors, Malcolm Gladwell and Seth Godin through his roles as a podcaster and interviewer with a Toronto-based conference production company.

Michael is an avid supporter of The Terry Fox Foundation and its annual run every year to help fund cancer research.

He lives in Markham, Ontario with his wife, Mateya and two children.

To learn more about Michael, go to:

www.thesuccessfulbookkeeper.com/about

Made in the USA
Columbia, SC
29 October 2024

45177765R00089